About the Author

I am a chartered accountant working in general practice. Based in Oxfordshire but with clients located across the country, I deal predominantly with small businesses and individuals. I originally trained with KPMG, one of the largest accounting firms in the country, before moving into the 'real world' of industry, taking on a number of roles in both a large manufacturing company and smaller scale service businesses.

If you have any suggestions to make things easier for readers of future editions of this book, I would be very pleased to hear from you.

For more details about my practice, please see my website. Unlike traditional High Street accountants, I can usually deal with most UK tax problems wherever you are located.

Contact details

Website   http://www.jamesesmith.co.uk
Email: contact@jamesesmith.co.uk

GW00506637

Dedication

To my grandparents, for your guidance and encouragement.

Taxcafe.co.uk Tax Guides

Keeping it Simple

*Small Business Bookkeeping,
Self Assessment and VAT*

By James Smith BSc ACA

Important Legal Notices:

Taxcafe®
TAX GUIDE – 'Keeping it Simple - Small Business Bookkeeping, Self Assessment and VAT'

Published by:
Taxcafe UK Limited
67 Milton Road
Kirkcaldy KY1 1TL
United Kingdom
Tel: (01592) 560081

First Edition   November 2007
Second Edition June 2008

ISBN 1 904608 82 5

Copyright

Trademarks

Disclaimer

Contents

Contents (cont ...)

Introduction

The purpose of this guide is to help owners of small businesses keep basic accounting records, complete a self-assessment tax return and understand VAT.

The bookkeeping and accounting chapters start by going over the basics of record keeping for sole traders and gradually build to take account of your legal responsibilities and information needs.

The self-assessment section takes a guinea pig taxpayer and shows how the four 'self-employment' tax return pages can be completed with minimum fuss.

The VAT section starts at ground level, showing you how VAT operates and helping you decide whether to register voluntarily or wait until you are forced to do so. The book gives practical pointers on how to register for VAT and what VAT scheme options exist to help you. The book ends with some suggested strategies you can use to get the most out of the VAT system.

The earlier sections of the book are useful when you are just starting up. Some of the themes covered later on will probably only become relevant after your first year or two of trading.

Section 1

Basic Bookkeeping

Chapter 1

How to Keep Basic Records

Although each business must assess its own record needs, there are certain things that apply to all businesses and the following section sets out the fundamentals.

Separation of Business & Personal Accounts

If you have recently started a business the first thing you should do is open a business bank account. This may sound obvious if you have already done so but many people start off using their personal bank accounts. This makes your record keeping that much harder as you will later have to determine whether each transaction was for personal or business reasons and you are unable to control your accounts with good bank reconciliation.

Most banks offer free banking for start-ups, typically for 18 months and many throw in free advice and other perks. At the time of writing, Abbey and Alliance and Leicester were offering free banking with an internet/postal account, ideal for many small businesses that don't deal with cash. Some of the other banks such as HSBC and RBS are also moving down this route with 'remote banking' accounts available at a much lower cost than traditional branch-based accounts. If you like to bank over the counter these accounts won't, however, be suitable for you.

Records of Your Income

Different businesses receive income from different sources. However, the basic principle does not change: you should keep good records that summarise your sources of income.

For a service company that sends out invoices, this record would simply be a list of invoices issued, as depicted in Figure 1.1

Figure 1.1 Income Spreadsheet

Ref	Description	Date	Amount
INV001	Mr A	01/01/2008	1,000.00
INV002	Mr C	02/01/2008	250.00
Total			1,250.00

- 'Ref' is the sequential and unique invoice number.
- 'Description' gives the client name and possibly the work completed.
- 'Date' is the invoice date.
- 'Amount' is the total invoice value.

A good idea is to keep a copy of all the invoices in a ring binder, in sequential order, detailing the work completed. The above spreadsheet would be your summary accounting record.

For a retail business, totals of the daily or weekly till receipts may be appropriate. The following sections discuss in more detail how to amend the basic record above for your own specific business needs, so don't worry too much if the above layout is inappropriate.

Retaining Your Receipts

A receipt is proof that you bought something. HM Revenue & Customs (the new name for Inland Revenue) may require this proof to be produced if you are ever investigated. You can submit secondary evidence, such as proof the payment went through your bank account or credit card statement, but you should not rely too heavily on this method of record keeping.

Keeping Your Receipts in Order

If you just throw your receipts in a carrier bag and hope for the best you will always struggle to keep good accounting records. The first step towards improving your records is to convert your carrier bag into some sense of order.

For example:

- Sort out your receipts into rough date order or by month.
- Number them with a thick marker pen starting with '1' for your earliest receipt. Keep this numbering system running forward so every receipt has a unique number on (say) the top right corner.
- Clip together a bundle of receipts (in numerical order) for every week or month.
- Put each bundle in a separate clear plastic wallet to stop them getting lost. It is helpful to indicate on the outside of the wallet the range of receipt numbers.
- Place in a box file or binder.

Processing Your Receipts

Now that you've got your receipts in order it's time to process them using a basic computer spreadsheet or manual accounts book. You may choose to use some accounting software but this will probably be overdoing it if you are just starting out. Figure 1.2 shows the layout for two example purchases: stationery for keeping your records and this book.

Figure 1.2 Expenses Spreadsheet

No.	Date	Payee	Description	Amount	Stationery	Books	Other
1	05/01/2008	Staples	Office Supplies	59.50	59.50		
2	06/01/2008	Taxcafe	Books	24.95		24.95	
				-			
				-			
				-			
				84.45	59.50	24.95	-

- In the first column 'No.' is the receipt number you have written in the top right corner when putting your receipts in order.
- 'Date' is the date of the invoice.
- 'Payee' is the person you bought the item from.
- 'Description' is the type of item you purchased.
- 'Amount' is the amount of the invoice you paid out (VAT is covered in later sections).
- There are now three further columns 'Stationery', 'Books' and 'Other'. These columns are there to describe the *type* of expenditure you incur and are very powerful and one of the keys to keeping good records.

Over time you will end up with a long list of expenses. Using this spreadsheet you will be able to:

- Easily see your total expenditure.

- See the total spend in a period for any type of item, such as stationery, by looking at the total at the bottom of the relevant column. You can insert subtotals to monitor the weekly or monthly performance.

- Find information. If you know you spent money on stationery, for example, but can't recall who the supplier was, you can quickly review the relevant analysis column and find the supplier and price.

- Find a given invoice. All you need do is find the relevant invoice number in the first column. Assuming you have marked up your invoices in numerical sequence and placed them in a box file they should be easy to retrieve without hours of searching.

- Save money. If instead of typing up your expenses yourself you give them to an accountant, he will charge you for this service. Rates vary widely depending on what firm you use and where you live. However, it is not unusual to pay between £15 and £30 an hour to have an accountancy firm type up your expenses.

Important: This section is fundamental to keeping good records. If you aren't happy with the basic principles listed above I strongly recommend you stop and go back over this section again, perhaps completing some worked examples using your own records. The following sections build on a basic working understanding of the above.

Chapter 2

Basic Accounting Controls

This chapter outlines the basic controls or 'checks and balances' that you can use to make sure your accounts are accurate.

Without controls it is very easy for your accounts to become inaccurate and unreliable. Good controls provide 'control loops' that ensure all entries are complete and accurate.

This might sound complex but it is actually straightforward if you take time and are patient about entering your data.

The only real difference between good and bad bookkeeping is the check procedures to ensure mistakes in data entry are quickly spotted and resolved.

Batch Totals

A batch total can be used to check that a group of figures (for example, your monthly expenses) is entered correctly into your accounting records.

In Chapter 1 I outlined a way to keep your receipts bundled – one bundle for every month. By adding up all the invoices in any particular month with a calculator, you can check if this figure matches the total amount appearing in your spreadsheet.

This is your batch total.

I always keep a printed copy of the spreadsheet, listing all the expenses, on the front of my invoice batches. This serves as a useful quick reference.

The more invoices you have the more important this type of procedure is to ensure you don't miss something or make a typing error.

A batch procedure may go something like this:

- Gather up the purchase invoices for the month as described in Chapter 1.
- Enter the invoices into your accounting records, for example using a spreadsheet.
- Add up all the invoices you've typed up (programs like Microsoft Excel let you do this automatically).
- Using a calculator add up all the paper invoices manually to check if the totals are the same.
- If there are any differences between the spreadsheet and the calculator:
  - Print out your spreadsheet for the period showing all the expenses.
  - Tick off line by line the invoices appearing in the spreadsheet against the paper invoices in your batch. As they are (hopefully!) in the same order this should be pretty painless and you will quickly see where the errors are.

Bank Reconciliations

Bank reconciliations are the fundamental control within any accounts system. They ensure that everything that has gone through the bank account is reflected somewhere in the accounts, even if it is in the wrong place. It is, therefore, helpful to get into the habit of doing regular bank reconciliations.

To complete accurate bank reconciliations you need two basic things:

- A separate business bank account so that only business transactions go through the account.
- Good accounting records showing the income and expenditure in the period.

The best time to complete a bank reconciliation is once a month when your bank statement arrives in the post. The worst time to do one is at the end of the financial year, having not completed one all year.

'Little and often' is the golden rule of good business bookkeeping.

Figure 2.1 shows how a simple bank reconciliation would look.

Figure 2.1 Bank Reconciliation

Opening bank balance as at 1st January 2008	500.00
Less purchases in the period	(84.45)
Add sales Income in the period	1,250.00
Closing balance expected 31st January 2008	1,665.55
Actual balance on the bank statement	1,660.55
Difference	(5.00)

We take the opening balance from the last time a reconciliation was completed (in this case the 1st of January), deduct the known purchases listed in the expenses spreadsheet, add the sales income from the sales spreadsheet and calculate an expected closing balance.

Looking at the actual balance on the bank statement you can see that the totals don't quite match up. Now £5 might not sound like much but there could be several things going wrong both ways – in other words, missed income AND missed expenditure.

First, take a good look at your bank statement. Figure 2.2 is a sample bank statement which contains the following transactions:

Figure 2.2 Bank Statement

Any Bank Account			Payments	Receipts	Balance
1 Jan 2008	Brought Forward				500.00
7 Jan 2008	Switch		59.50		440.50
9 Jan 2008	Switch		24.95		415.55
15 Jan 2008	Cheque			1,000.00	1,415.55
17 Jan 2008	Cheque			250.00	1,665.55
19 Jan 2008	Cheque			100.00	1,765.55
22 Jan 2008	Transfer		105.00		1,660.55
31 Jan 2008	Closing Balance				1,660.55

At this point a lot of people give up, especially in a real-life scenario where the bank statement contains dozens of items and the apparent difference is very small. However, if your records have been prepared as described above, you should be able to quickly find the problem.

First, compare the payments in your bank statement with the list of expenses on your spreadsheet.

You can quickly tick off the £59.50 and the £24.95 but there is also a mystery payment of £105 on the 22 January. You quickly realise that this amount was money taken out as a 'drawing'.

Drawings are amounts taken personally by the owner of a sole trader business. Strictly speaking they are not a business expense, but recording them on your expenses sheet makes sense for bookkeeping purposes.

You therefore go back and amend the 'expenses' spreadsheet adding a descriptive column for 'drawings' (Figure 2.3)

Figure 2.3 Expenses Spreadsheet

No.	Date	Payee	Description	Amount	Stationery	Books	Drawings
1	05/01/2008	Staples	Office Supplies	59.50	59.50		
2	06/01/2008	Taxcafe	Books	24.95		24.95	
3	08/01/2008	Self	Drawings	105.00			105.00
				-			
				-			
				189.45	59.50	24.95	105.00

A similar review of the sales income shows a mystery cheque for £100 deposited in the bank. Then you recall that you had completed three items of work in January and had forgotten to list the third invoice and update the sales list accordingly.

The revised reconciliation is as follows (Figure 2.4):

Figure 2.4 Bank Reconciliation

Opening bank balance as at 1st January 2008	500.00
Less purchases in the period	(189.45)
Add sales income in the period	1,350.00
Closing balance expected 31st January 2008	1,660.55
Actual balance on the bank statement	1,660.55
Difference	0.00

There is now no difference showing between the bank statement and the spreadsheet and the accounts are therefore fully reconciled.

Sometimes there are genuine differences between your cash position and what is shown in your accounts.

Typical reasons for this would be:

- Sales invoices that haven't been paid yet.
- Things you have bought but not paid for yet.
- Cheques you have paid into the bank account but haven't cleared.
- Personal items purchased from the business account.
- Business items purchased from private funds.

In these circumstances you may have some 'reconciling items'.

Some of these, such as invoices not yet paid and uncleared cheques, will be 'reversing' items. In other words, what is a reconciling item one month will be cleared the next.

Other items, such as mixing private and business money, will be permanent and you should record these as you go along.

Most reconciliation problems can be dealt with by applying a little logic and if you get into the routine of reconciling your bank account every month you will learn how to deal with the occasional oddity or missed transaction.

If you struggle to complete your bank reconciliation don't be afraid to get some help. Bank reconciliations are probably the most troublesome problem people face with basic bookkeeping, but are certainly worth doing as they help ensure your records are accurate.

Check Totals

Check totals can be used to make sure all the individual expense columns add up correctly.

In the example expenses layout in Figure 2.3, the total of the 'Amount' column should be the same as the total of all the individual analysis columns. In other words, the total of the 'Stationery' column (£59.50) plus 'Books' (£24.95) plus Drawings (£105) equals the total of the 'Amount' column £189.45.

Spreadsheet Tip

You can use a check formula to add up the sum of all the analysis columns and check this is the same as the total of the 'Amount' column. If you put this formula just under the total of the Amount column (see Figure 2.5) it will alert you where there is a difference.

Figure 2.5 Looking for Counting Errors

	A	B	C	D	E	F	G	H
1								
2	No.	Date	Payee	Description	Amount	Stationery	Books	Drawings
3								
4	1	05/01/2008	Staples	Office Supplies	59.50	59.50		
5	2	06/01/2008	Taxcafe	Books	24.95		24.95	
6	3	22/01/2008	Self	Drawings	105.00			105.00
7								
8					189.45	59.50	24.95	105.00
9								
10					0			

In this example the spreadsheet formula would be:

=sum(E4:E7) − sum(F8:H8)

If the number in the box is not zero you can immediately see something is wrong with your analysis.

If you're using manual books you will have to manually add up the column totals and check this comes back to the total of the 'Amount'. Typically you would do that at the bottom of each page as you go on through your accounts book.

Chapter 3

How to Send Out Invoices That Get Paid!

A common question from owners of new businesses is: "How do I lay out an invoice?" I have put together some examples for both a simple sole trader and a VAT-registered limited company – the latter is discussed more fully in later sections of this book.

Do I Need an Invoice?

Not all businesses issue invoices. If you deal in retail where the customer buys goods 'over the counter' using cash or a credit card, you normally just issue a till receipt. Similarly, many online businesses that deal only with consumer items don't give out invoices.

Principally you need to provide an invoice if:

- You get paid *after* you supply the goods or services.
- You are dealing with other businesses and they require a proper invoice to be raised.

What Should I Include on My Invoice?

Your invoice should contain the same details as your headed paper. The details for headed paper are set out in Appendix 1.

In addition, you must include the following information:

- The word 'Invoice'
- The date of the invoice

A basic invoice for a non-VAT-registered service company may look similar to the example one in Figure 3.1.

Figure 3.1 A Sample Invoice

Company Name			Address Line 1
			Address Line 2
LOGO			Address Line 3
		Telephone	01234 567890
Billing Address			
Mr A			**Invoice**
Address Line 1			
Address Line 2		Invoice Ref	INV001
Address Line 3		Invoice Date	01/01/2008
Address Line 4			

Qty	Description		Total (£)
2	Weasels	£	800.00
1	Badger	£	200.00
		Total	£ **1,000.00**

You must include your name and address and that of the customer, the invoice number, date and a list of the items sold.

If you are selling lots of multiple items you may like to have an additional column showing the price per item and the quantity of each item.

More Complex Invoices

If you are VAT-registered you need to include the following additional information:

- The VAT element of the invoice should be clearly stated.
- The rate of VAT, normally 17.5%.
- The date of supply or 'tax point' (this is explored in more detail in the VAT section below).

I also strongly suggest you include the following so that customers can pay you easily:

- Payment terms (14 days, 30 days etc).
- Due date of the invoice.
- Payment instructions, i.e. the name of the person/company to whom any cheques are payable, plus your bank account details for direct payments plus any reference details required.
- Contact name and number for any queries.

These bits of information are included to help your customers pay you as quickly as possible. I don't know about you, but I'm always put off paying an invoice if I first have to ring up to ask to whom my cheque should be made payable or to get hold of the bank account details.

Many businesses now make all their payments via electronic or internet banking, so not including your details seems rather amateurish, not to mention rather damaging to your cash flow if you are put to the bottom of the pile.

The same invoice for a VAT-registered business would look something like Figure 3.2. I have incorporated the additional payment information in a box at the bottom.

Spreadsheet Tip

If you are using spreadsheet software to generate your invoices, it is straightforward to enter one date as the 'invoice date' and let the 'due date' and 'tax point' be calculated automatically with a simple formula. Similarly, you should be able to get your spreadsheet to work out the VAT for you automatically once you have entered the line totals.

Figure 3.2 Sample Invoice – VAT Included

Billing Address		Invoice	
Mr A			
Address Line 1			
Address Line 2		Invoice Ref	INV001
Address Line 3		Invoice Date	01/01/2008
Address Line 4		Tax Point	01/01/2008
		Terms	14 Days
		DUE DATE	**15/01/2008**

Qty	Description		Total (£)	
2	Weasels		£	800.00
1	Badger		£	200.00
		Sub Total	£	1,000.00
		Vat @ 17.5%		175.00
		TOTAL	£	**1,175.00**

Payment Details

This invoice is **due for payment by the 15th January 2008**
Payment should be made to Bank Name account no. 12345678, sort code 00-00-00
Cheques should be made payable to "Company Name" and sent to the above address

Company Trading Name is the trading name of Company Legal Name Ltd
Registered in England No. 01234567. VAT registration number 123456789

From a VAT point of view we can see the addition of the tax point (normally the same as the invoice date) and the VAT amounts clearly listed.

If some of the items you are selling are subject to VAT and others are not, you will either have to issue separate invoices for the different items or add two new columns for 'VAT' and 'Gross' so that the VAT element on each item is clearly shown. This won't apply to most readers.

From a credit control point of view we can see the payment details listed quite prominently with the due date in the payment details box. This should help with this document's main purpose – getting your business paid for the goods or services provided.

By now you should have a good idea what to include on your invoices. It's worth looking at the invoices other people send you and thinking about what works and what doesn't in the context of your business. For example, if everyone pays you before you dispatch goods, then there is very little point including the payment instructions section that is crucial to many service businesses.

Chapter 4

What Records the Taxman Expects You to Keep

Why Keep Records?

To take your record keeping to the next level it helps to think about *why* you need to keep records. There are two principal reasons:

- To prepare your self-assessment tax return.
- For management purposes – in other words, to help you improve your business.

Preparing the self-assessment return is probably what most sole traders are concerned about but creating your own management accounts, with which you can measure the performance of your business and identify any problems, is just as important.

Successful businesses tend to integrate their accounting systems and their operational ones. This may sound complicated but it can be as simple as using the same spreadsheet to record income for accounts purposes as you do for recording which of your invoices remain unpaid.

By having one set of documents that are central to your business you can reduce the chances of errors or omissions. If your record keeping is an afterthought it will tend to result in problems in the longer term.

As a small sole trader the requirements for record keeping are not nearly as onerous as for a limited company or larger enterprise. This section details the types of information you will need to record and retain so that you can complete your self assessment tax return at the end of the year.

There are three basic classes of information you need to record.

Class of Information	Basic Requirements
Sales	Total sales income received. Evidence of completeness of sales.
Expenses	All business expenses by statutory category with supporting invoices as evidence.
Stock	Value of opening and closing stocks on hand.

Sales

The basic record-keeping procedure described in Chapter 1 will generally be sufficient for most small businesses. As you will recall, this simply involves listing all invoices you have sent out, backed up by the invoices themselves or the invoice book.

You should also record any invoices that remain unpaid at the year-end, especially if you do not expect to receive any payment.

Some businesses do not send invoices if they deal mainly with cash or earn commissions. In this instance retain the till rolls or commission statements as evidence of your income.

You may prefer to group daily or weekly payments rather than list a large number of small items. This is perfectly acceptable, provided you have the full information available for inspection by the taxman.

If you have a cash business, the completeness of your records may well be questioned. Ideally, bank your takings daily or weekly so the money can be seen arriving in your business bank account. This will be helpful in the long run, especially if you can show all payments received are traceable through the bank account.

Expenses

If your business has a turnover of less than £2,500 per month (£30,000 per year) you can report your expenses as a single lump sum on your tax return. There is no legal requirement to split them up into different categories.

Businesses with a turnover in excess £2,500 per month are required to split their expenses up into certain 'statutory' categories.

Revenue & Customs guidance detailing what expenses to include in each category is contained in Appendix 2. The categories include:

- Costs of goods bought for re-sale
- Wages, salaries and other staff costs
- Car, van and travel expenses
- Rent, rates, power and insurance costs
- Repair and renewals of property and equipment
- Telephone, fax, stationery and other office costs
- Advertising and business entertainment
- Interest on bank and other loans
- Bank, credit card and other financial charges
- Irrecoverable debts written off
- Accountancy, legal and other professional fees
- Depreciation and loss/profit on sale of assets
- Other business expenses

Earlier we saw how expenses could be put into different categories. In choosing which categories to use you should try to ensure you don't put together expenses that need to be shown separately on your tax return.

For example, you might quite reasonably have a category called 'Office' and record all your office expenses within this category, including paying the office rent and insurance. At year-end you will find 'Rent, rates and power and insurance' and 'Telephone, fax stationery and other office costs' are *separate* categories. You will then have to go back and split up a year's worth of transactions.

Problems like this are easy to avoid with a bit of forward planning. Simply split up your expenses into the relevant statutory categories and you'll keep the taxman happy! It's probably worth having a look through the categories now to see which ones apply to your business.

Some sole traders set up their accounts using only the statutory categories. However, as we will see below, it can be a good idea, from a management information perspective, to have subcategories.

You may wish to analyse 'Telephone', 'Website Costs', 'Stationery' and 'Other Office Expenses', all of which are reported on your tax return under the single statutory category: 'Telephone, fax, stationery and other office costs'.

There's a potentially big difference between 'management accounting' and 'financial accounting'. Management accounting is all about using accounting information to help you run your business more efficiently and make it more profitable. This type of information is often kept confidential so that competitors do not get their hands on it.

Financial accounting, on the other hand, is all about complying with rules and regulations: completing your tax return and producing annual accounts (if your business is run through a company).

Stock

If your business has stock (in other words, if it sells goods rather than services) you must keep a record of the stock on hand at the end of the financial year. A simple stock count will normally suffice. If you have large volumes of low-value items, estimates are permitted based on, for example, weight or physical volume.

Note that stock is valued at cost rather than sales price.

Checklist of Records to Keep

The following is a checklist of the information you need to retain for proper accounting records. You need to keep this information for up to six years:

- Purchase receipts or other evidence of purchases
- Sales invoices or other evidence of income
- Closing stock records at year end
- Company bank statements
- Paying-in books and cheque book stubs
- Your summary accounting records

Don't be tempted to throw these things out if your business closes. A few boxes at the back of your garage or in your loft may well save a lot of problems if you are ever the subject of a Revenue and Customs investigation.

Registration of a Sole Trader or Partnership

You are required to register your sole trader business (or partnership) with Revenue and Customs within three months of 'commencement of trade'.

The relevant form is a 'CWF1', which can be downloaded from the HMRC website: www.hmrc.gov.uk/forms/cwf1.pdf

Another easy way to register is by calling the newly self-employed helpline 08459 154515, so Revenue and Customs can guide you through the process. Details are on the website:

www.hmrc.gov.uk/startingup

This registration serves two purposes:

- It puts you in the 'self-assessment' tax system so you will automatically receive a tax return and reminders.

- It allows HMRC to deduct Class 2 National Insurance of £2.30 per week, which every self-employed business pays unless your earnings are below £5,435 per annum in the 2008/9 tax year.

Establishing when commencement of trade takes place isn't a precise science. It's basically when your doors are open for business – whether anyone comes in is another matter! There are fines for failure to register in a timely manner, so make sure you look into this if you weren't aware of the need to register.

Where to Go From Here

This first section should have helped you appreciate some of the basic bookkeeping requirements of a small sole trader business.

For many readers, especially those just starting out in business, this should be more than sufficient for now.

Others may be feeling a bit shell-shocked and in need of a good cup of tea! If this is you, it may help to put this book away and read it again tomorrow, perhaps using your own information to go through the Basic Bookkeeping section before reading on any further.

Don't be too disheartened if you still aren't happy with your records. This section is not exhaustive and will not suit everyone's methods of learning and business situation and, quite frankly, not everyone wants to do their own bookkeeping.

Suggested Next Steps

- Re-read this section at least once.

- Try to identify what your reporting needs are.

- Jot down the types of expenses you have and the ones you want to keep an eye on.

- Set out a basic structure for your accounts, along the lines discussed above.

- Put your receipts and income in a logical order (probably date order).

- Start filling in your records, for example using a spreadsheet listing all your expenses.

- Adjust your record structure as your needs change. Your first ideas will probably need to be refined a number of times during the first 12 months as the business develops.

- When you receive your bank statement, remember to reconcile it. Don't try to do more than one month at a time – the more transactions; the harder it is to perform.

Section 2

Introducing VAT

Chapter 5

How VAT Works in Plain English

If VAT is new to you, read on! This chapter will help you understand the basics, even if you don't intend to register right now.

Businesses are not automatically VAT registered so if you haven't applied for and obtained a VAT number you won't be currently registered for VAT.

Chapter 25, "Should I Register for VAT?", explores in more detail whether voluntary registration is suitable for your business and how to go about it. Registration is compulsory if your turnover exceeds the VAT threshold, which is £67,000 for 2008/9.

So what exactly is VAT?

- Value Added Tax (VAT) is charged on the supply of most good and services.

- The standard VAT rate is 17.5%.

- Only VAT-registered companies charge VAT on their sales.

- Only VAT-registered companies can reclaim VAT on their costs.

- VAT-registered companies administer and collect VAT on behalf of HM Revenue and Customs, the government body responsible for VAT.

17.5% of What Exactly?

The quoted rate of 17.5% is applied to the net value of an invoice. So if a VAT-registered company wants to receive a net price of £100 it will add a further 17.5% VAT and sell the item at £117.50.

Example

Net value of invoice	£100.00
VAT at 17.5%	£ 17.50
Gross value of invoice	£117.50

If the company wishes to sell at a total price of £100 the net selling price is found by dividing the gross price by 1.175.

For example:

Gross value of invoice	£100.00
Net value of the invoice (£100/1.175)	£ 85.11
Vat (£85.11 multiplied by 17.5%)	£ 14.89

Taxcafe's free VAT calculator lets you perform calculations such as these at the touch of a button. It is available at:

http://www.taxcafe.co.uk/vatcalc

Now we can calculate VAT, it is helpful to see how it works in practice.

Example

Tom chops down trees for a living and is VAT registered.

Tom sells £1,000 of wood to Dick and gives him an invoice for £1,175 (£1,000 plus £175 VAT).

Dick pays Tom the total amount of £1,175. Tom keeps £1,000 and pays £175 to Revenue and Customs when he submits his VAT return.

Dick is a furniture maker and also VAT registered. He takes the £1,000 worth of wood and makes a table for Harry. Harry is the end consumer and has agreed to pay a total of £3,525 for the table.

Dick gets his calculator out and works out that if Harry is prepared to pay £3,525 in total, he must charge him £3,000 plus VAT of £525.

Appearing on Dick's VAT return will be £525 of 'output tax' (the VAT on his sales). This money has to be paid to Revenue and Customs.

Dick also has £175 'input tax' (the VAT on the wood he bought from Tom). This money has to be <u>claimed back</u> from Revenue and Customs.

The difference between his output tax and his input tax – £350 – is the actual amount paid over to the VAT man.

On Dick's income tax return he will ignore VAT and declare net sales of £3,000 and net purchases of £1,000, resulting in a profit of £2,000.

The VAT man has received £175 from Tom and £350 from Dick. This is the same as the total VAT of £525 paid by Harry. However, Harry doesn't pay the VAT man directly – instead Tom and Dick effectively take on the role of tax collectors.

In other businesses the same principles apply – VAT-registered companies collect VAT and pass it on to Revenue and Customs.

Who Really Ends Up Paying the Tax?

If a business is VAT registered it can claim back all the tax it has paid on its expenses, so there is no real financial loss.

But if your business is not VAT registered you cannot claim back any VAT you pay so there is a real financial loss. Everything you buy from VAT-registered businesses will cost 17.5% more.

What about your income and sales – who really pays the VAT on the invoices you send out? If you send a VAT invoice to a VAT-registered business, that business doesn't care because it knows it can reclaim that VAT.

But if you send an invoice to a business that is not registered, or if your customer is a private individual, the VAT represents a real added cost because the tax cannot be recovered by the customer.

The critical question now is who really pays the tax: your business or your customer?

If you were able to sell 100 widgets for £100 before you were VAT registered and can still sell 100 widgets for £100 + £17.50 VAT after registering, then it is your customer who is worse off – you have managed to pass the entire VAT cost on to him.

However, if after registering for VAT you can only sell 100 widgets for £85.11 + £14.89 VAT then it is your business that is worse off – you have not managed to pass on any of the VAT cost to your customers (perhaps because there are competitors out there who are not VAT registered and can still sell 100 widgets for £100).

Chapter 6

VAT Jargon Demystified

It is important to get to grips with the following basic VAT terminology:

Inputs	The value of the goods and services <u>received or purchased</u> by your business, i.e. goods in.
Input VAT	The value of the VAT on the inputs
Outputs	The value of the goods or services <u>supplied or sold</u> by your business, i.e. goods out.
Output VAT	The value of the VAT on the outputs

Non-standard VAT Rates

No doubt you have come across invoices that don't have any VAT on them or the VAT is at a reduced rate (for example, the VAT rate on electricity bills is 5%). This may be because the business that sends out the invoice is either VAT exempt or sells 'zero-rated' products.

VAT-exempt Firms

Some firms do not have to add VAT to their invoices. This may be because they are under the VAT registration threshold or because they supply services that are VAT exempt. For example, banks do not levy VAT on many of their charges.

Although they don't need to charge VAT, exempt firms cannot reclaim VAT on their purchases, so it isn't always a great position to be in.

Zero-rated Firms

Zero-rated firms are those that don't have to charge any VAT on their sales but can reclaim the VAT paid on expenses. As it happens these firms do theoretically charge VAT on their sales but at the rate of 0%! This means they are permanently receiving VAT refunds for the tax paid on their expenses.

Typical zero-rated businesses are those that sell food (but not meals in restaurants or hot take-aways), bookshops and publishers, suppliers of children's clothing and shoes and exporters.

If you do sell zero-rated items it makes sense to register for VAT so that you can reclaim all the VAT on your expenses without having to charge any VAT to your customers.

VAT on Imports and Exports of Goods

Non-registered Companies

If you are not VAT registered and make goods purchases from other EU countries then you will simply pay any VAT added to your purchases.

For goods arriving from outside the EU, VAT will possibly be added (if the country where you're buying from has VAT or some other sales tax) and you may also have to pay import duty if you are buying physical goods.

VAT-registered Companies

If your business is VAT registered you can make European goods purchases free of VAT if you provide your VAT number before the invoice is sent out to you.

Similarly, your sales to European countries can be zero rated if you obtain your customer's VAT details. You cannot, however, reclaim overseas VAT paid when you submit your VAT return.

If you're making purchases outside the EU, if the company has your VAT number you will normally only have to pay import duty without the added cost of VAT.

Duties with the US in particular can be significant, so remember to check how much you could pay before placing any orders.

Import & Export Tips

- When selling in the EU and charging no VAT, quote the purchaser's VAT number on your invoice to prove you have obtained it.

- EU VAT can sometimes be reclaimed using a specialist European VAT reclaim service. This may be worthwhile if you travel frequently to Europe on business. The rules vary considerably, however.

- For example, if you happen to be at a conference in one country you may be able to reclaim VAT on your hotel, meals and conference tickets.

  In another country you may only be able to reclaim the VAT on your conference ticket, and in another the VAT on your accommodation may be reclaimed but you won't get any VAT back on your meals.

  Individual circumstances need to be looked at carefully to determine if a claim is worthwhile. You can find a selection of companies offering a VAT reclaim service by going to Google and typing "EU VAT Reclaim".

Summary Table

	Imports (Goods Purchases)	Export (Goods Sales)
EU - Not Registered	Overseas VAT added to your purchases.	No VAT.
EU - Registered	Provide your VAT number to your supplier to be invoiced with no European VAT.	You must include VAT on your sales unless the purchaser provides you with a European VAT number. You may then invoice without any VAT.
World	VAT added by customs to physical imports unless a VAT number supplied to your import agent.	No VAT chargeable on your invoice. Local taxes may apply in the export country.

VAT on Imports and Exports of Services

If you are a VAT registered company providing services to other EU countries or worldwide, there is an extra complication known as the 'place of supply' rules.

These rules are rather fiendish in detail but broadly what they aim to do is levy VAT, not where the end customer is, but where the business 'belongs', in other words where the service is actually performed. In practice this means that if you are a service business you may still have to charge UK VAT for services provided to customers outside the UK.

There are an awful lot of specific rules in this area, principally concerning land, transport and broadcast media, but also covering a large number of other areas.

Example

Claire provides proof reading services for scientific papers. Her customers are based in the UK, US and in Poland. As the place of supply (where the work is performed) is the UK, she must charge UK VAT not only to her non-VAT registered Polish customers but also to her US customers. Had she been selling goods she would not have charged VAT to the US.

Matters do become quite complex when it comes to electronic media and if you have a service based internet business you will need to take some detailed advice in this area.

If you deal with items that are physically present in other countries it is even possible to end up paying overseas VAT.

Example 2

Claire decides to organise a large scientific conference in Poland and receives money from ticket sales in both the UK and Poland. As the place of supply is deemed to be the location of the conference, and not where her business 'belongs', she is somewhat surprised to find a Polish VAT officer demanding that she pays over Polish VAT on the ticket sales!

For more details on this topic please see Notice 741 on the Revenue and Customs website. The direct web address is too long to reproduce here but if you type the phrase "VAT place of supply" into Google you should find it relatively easily. I should point out that, as a general accountant rather than a VAT specialist, even I have to take advice on this topic from time to time and I would suggest that you do the same if necessary.

Section 3

How Good Accounts Help a Business Grow

Chapter 7

Introduction

This section develops the themes from the Basic Bookkeeping section. If you've jumped straight in here, you may find it worthwhile flicking through the previous section to ensure you haven't missed anything.

Obviously I can't cover all eventualities and business types in a guide such as this. For example, for a business that earns all its income from large companies and is paid three months after invoice date, credit control and cash flow are going to be very important.

Credit control is not an issue where all income is received before delivery. To get most benefit from reading this book you need to think about your own specific business needs.

To help you do this we'll take a look at two case studies in the next two chapters, the first involving James who sells e-books online, the second involving Emily who sells works of art.

James sells his e-books on his own website and on E-bay. He has a large number of small sales that are paid for in advance using PayPal, the well-known online payment company.

Emily sells a small number of art works purchased from third parties. She holds some items in stock and clients pay her by cheque.

Their management accounting needs are somewhat more involved than their needs for tax purposes and each will require different information.

Chapter 8

Case Study 1: James's Bookshop

The following table (Figure 8.1) summarises James's basic accounting information requirements:

Figure 8.1 Why James Needs Accounts

For Tax Purposes	For Management Purposes
• Total sales in the year	• Sales by time period (week/month) • Sales by book title
• Expenses by statutory category with supporting evidence	• Expense totals by type

Sales

James wants to know how much he makes in total each week from selling e-books, which titles are selling and which are not. He'd also like to know where the books are sold (on his website or on eBay). He doesn't really want a detailed list of all sales, as that would be too much information.

James doesn't send out invoices so the first question is, where does he source his accounting information? We know all sales (both from his website and from Ebay) are processed by PayPal, the online credit card payment processor. So this seems the logical place to start.

From PayPal he can obtain a weekly summary that lists the income and credit card processing charges between given dates. He could print this out every week and enter the information on a spreadsheet, like the one in Figure 8.2

Figure 8.2 James's Sales

Week	Description	Amount	Book 1	Book 2	Book 3
01/01/2008	eBay	1,000.00	250.00	150.00	600.00
01/08/2008	eBay	250.00	150.00	50.00	50.00
01/08/2008	Website	100.00	25.00	25.00	50.00
Total		1,350.00	425.00	225.00	700.00

- 'Week' now gives the week in which the sales occurred, rather than invoice numbers.
- 'Description' states the source of the income.
- 'Amount' shows the weekly sales income received.
- 'Book 1', 'Book 2', 'Book 3' show the sales of each of James's books.

These new analysis columns allow James to see which titles are doing well. Alternatively he may wish to record the number of sales instead of the value.

What works for your business only you can decide but it isn't hard to build extra 'management' information like this into your accounting records.

We can see that in the week starting January 8th James received some sales directly from his website and some from eBay. He has chosen to put two lines on the spreadsheet for January 8th to distinguish where his sales have come from.

This is where having the extra descriptive field comes in handy and using a basic spreadsheet set up more fields can be entered or removed as required.

From this very basic arrangement James can find out:

- In which week sales occurred
- Which titles are selling
- The source of the sale

It wouldn't take a lot of work to analyse this data in lots of different ways to help James spot trends and therefore improve the running of his business.

Expenses

James wants to know how much he is spending on eBay auction fees, PayPal credit card charges and general office expenditure. He uses the same basic layout that we used in Figure 2.3 earlier, with the revised headings as follows:

Figure 8.3 James's Expenses

No.	Date	Payee	Description	Amount	Stationery	PayPal	eBay
1	05/01/2008	Staples	Office Supplies	59.50	59.50		
2	06/01/2008	PayPal	Transaction Fees	8.99		8.99	
3	08/01/2008	eBay	Sellers Fees	105.00			105.00
4	09/01/2008	PayPal	Transaction Fees	8.50		8.50	
				-			
				181.99	59.50	17.49	105.00

Specific Points about eBay and PayPal Fees

For accounting purposes we need to show both the gross income (in other words, the total turnover before fees) and the full eBay and PayPal fees that have been charged.

For example, James may sell a book for £10 but only receive £9.00 in his PayPal account. Sales income would be shown as £10 gross and PayPal expenses of £1.00.

This can be a bit disconcerting at first, as you are creating two transactions from one amount, but you need to think about what has actually happened.

- James has sold an item at the full price of £10
- PayPal has charged him a merchant fee of £1

Had the merchant fee been charged at the end of the month you would be able to see the two underlying transactions clearly – an income and an expense.

The confusing thing about PayPal and other online transactions is that both transactions occur at the same time. You are in receipt of the net amount, rather than receiving the full sales income and then paying the charge at a later date.

Recognition of Sales

James needs to show in his accounts when sales are *earned* – when he makes a sale rather than when the cash is physically transferred into his business bank account.

If money is transferred from his PayPal account to his bank account on a weekly basis then treating the sales as having occurred on the date of transfer to his bank account will be just about acceptable, with a small year-end adjustment.

If, however, he uses his PayPal account for storing funds and perhaps for paying for other purchases, he may need to treat his PayPal account as he would any other business bank account and carry out reconciliations.

Taxable Transactions

There is unfortunately a lot of uninformed comment in the press about what is and isn't taxable when it comes to selling things on eBay.

The tax rules for eBay sales are the same as for any other business. If you are involved in a 'trade'– in other words if you buy and sell for a profit motive – then you are deemed to be 'trading' and your profits are taxable.

If you sell a few items that you originally purchased for your own use or were, say, given for Christmas, this is not trading and not taxable.

Chapter 9

Case Study 2: Emily's Art

Emily's business is more complex than James's. She buys and sells stock items (paintings) and is paid by cheque. Each customer is sent an invoice and only pays after this has been received. Figure 9.1 summarises Emily's basic information requirements.

Figure 9.1 Why Emily Needs Accounts

For Tax Purposes	For Management Purposes
• Total sales in the year	• Sales by time (week/month) • Sales by client • Profit per picture • Debtors – who owes money
• Expenses by statutory category with supporting evidence	• Expense totals by type of spend
• Stock on hand at year end	• Stock on hand by picture

Sales

Emily's two key management tasks are:

- Stock control (knowing how much stock should be held and how much should be ordered), and

- Ensuring each invoice is paid.

These tasks should determine how Emily designs her accounting records.

The sales spreadsheet may look something like Figure 9.2:

Figure 9.2 Emily's Sales

Ref	Invoice Date	Customer	Artist	Amount	Paid Date	Cost	Gross Profit
INV001	01/01/2008	Mr A	Anna	1,000.00	08/01/2008	700.00	300.00
INV002	02/01/2008	Mr C	Paul	250.00	22/01/2008	100.00	150.00
INV003	05/01/2008	Mrs D	Peter	100.00		25.00	75.00
Total				1,350.00		825.00	525.00

- 'Ref' - the invoice reference.
- 'Invoice date' - the date of the sale.
- 'Customer' - who has bought the picture.
- 'Artist' - which artist painted the piece.
- 'Amount' - the amount invoiced.

There are also some extra descriptive fields:

- 'Paid Date' shows the date the invoice was paid. This column is very useful to track whose payments are outstanding and help with the bank reconciliation. Using this column Emily can see quickly who still owes her for the paintings and take appropriate credit control action. For Emily this is very important. As we can see, Mrs D has not yet paid for the painting sent on January 5th and needs to be chased up.

- The 'Cost' and 'Gross Profit' columns are useful because they show how much has been made on each picture. Gross profit is simply sales minus costs of goods sold, so if Emily buys a picture for £100 and sells it for £250 her gross profit is £150. Gross profit does not take account of operating expenses such as stationery, telephone and office rent.

  If Emily had a large number of paintings, each at a standard mark-up, the gross profit number would be superfluous. Because she has a small number of items at varying mark-ups she can quickly see what her gross profits are for the period.

You could of course add extra fields to suit your needs, for example Emily could add the name of the piece of art or a list of paintings ordered but not yet invoiced.

The aim of management accounts is to allow *you* to run your business successfully and in doing so keep the paperwork to a minimum.

Expenses

Emily's requirements for recording expenses are no different to James's apart from the category titles, so I won't elaborate on this point.

Stock

Stock management is crucial to Emily's business so suitable records must be kept. There are many ways of doing this but a simple list such as the one in Figure 9.3 will suffice:

Figure 9.3 Emily's Stock Management

Date Purchased	Artist	Item Name	Purchase Price	Date Sold		Stock Value
01/12/2007	Anna	Flowers	700.00	01/01/2008		-
01/12/2007	Paul	Seascape	100.00	02/01/2008		-
01/12/2007	Peter	Calm	25.00	05/01/2008		-
01/12/2007	John	Face	400.00	Stock		400.00
	Total		1,225.00			400.00

The above spreadsheet contains the purchase date and purchase price, the date the item was sold and some descriptive columns for the supplier (the artist in this case) and item name (the name of the painting).

The Stock Value column can be linked to the Purchase Price column using a simple formula. For example, if the purchase price of the Face painting is stored in cell D7 of the spreadsheet, Emily could type '=D7' in the Stock Value column. The number '400' will then appear as it does above.

Then, when the Face painting is sold, she could simply replace the number 400 with a '0' or '-'. This way there is always a 'live' stock value.

By including the 'Date Sold' column it is always possible to go back and establish the stock level at an earlier date, if required for accounting purposes. It may also be possible to combine both the sales and stock pages on one sheet, although this could become a bit cumbersome.

If Emily was dealing with a large volume of similar items, for example, say she bought 5,000 postcards to sell, a different approach would be needed.

There are many ways of doing this. Figure 9.4 suggests a typical layout for a stock record with large volumes of identical items:

Figure 9.4 Stock Management – Large Volumes

Date	Description	Amount £	Sales £	Quantity	1	2	3
01/01/2008	Purchase - A	200.00	-	5,000	2,400	1,500	1,100
07/01/2008	Sales		(34.76)	(869)	(124)	(325)	(420)
14/01/2008	Sales		(11.28)	(282)	(27)	(25)	(230)
Total		200.00	(46.04)	3,849	2,249	1,150	450

- 'Date' gives the date of the transaction.
- 'Description' gives the type of transaction, either a purchase of stock or a sale.
- 'Amount' gives the amount paid for the stock.
- 'Sales' is the *cost of goods sold*, based on an average unit cost of 4p per unit (5,000 cards bought for £200). In this example 4p is the known cost of the stock.
- 'Quantity' is the physical quantity of cards purchased or sold.
- '1, 2, 3' give the stock levels of each design.

Using this approach you can quickly see the level of each stock item without manually checking your stock levels. You also have some idea of the level of transactions to enable you to plan your stock replenishment.

Again real-life examples may be more or less complex than this example and if you deal with a lot of stock you may find upgrading to a proper accounting system is preferable.

This is particularly useful if you have a large range of items with different prices and mark-ups that is too complex for a simple spreadsheet.

If you're a small trader, setting out your accounts as described above will give you a basic structure to get you started. You can then build and adapt this as your business needs dictate.

Section 4

How to Complete Your Tax Return Without Fuss

Chapter 10

Business Tax Return Basics

In this section I will show you how to prepare the self employment pages of your tax return.

This is by no means an exhaustive explanation and is designed to show you how the accounting information discussed above fits into your return.

Even if you have no intention of completing your tax return yourself and would prefer an accountant to do it for you, it's well worth reading this section so that you understand where the numbers you produce for your business end up and why certain things in your accounts are important.

Know your Dates

The first thing you need to know is the date your return has to be completed.

- The tax year runs from April 6th to April 5th the following year.
- The tax year ending on April 5th 2008 is generally denoted 2007/8.
- Payments for the period to April 5th 2008 have to be made by the 31st January 2009.
- Paper tax returns for 2007/8 should be submitted by the 31st October 2008 although in practice there should be no fine so long as you file your return and pay any tax due by the 31st January 2009.
- Electronic returns for 2007/8 have to be submitted by the 31st January 2009.

Remember, however long you've got, it's never too early to make a start on your tax return.

The longer you leave it, the less chance you have of getting help from either an accountant or Revenue and Customs. Furthermore, returns completed at the last minute are more likely to lead to higher tax bills, given the tendency of most people to err on the side of caution.

Tip: Early filing will give you earlier conclusion of your affairs. Revenue and Customs must open an enquiry into your return within 12 months of the date of your having submitted it, the 'enquiry window', so the sooner you file the sooner you will have certainty of your affairs.

Tip: The online filing system doesn't cope too well with the 31st January rush, so you will avoid a lot of frustration if you start to think about completing your self assessment return when you are still mowing the grass rather than whilst taking down the Christmas decorations.

What Period?

There is a general concession that allows sole traders to draw up their accounts to March 31st instead of April 5th.

For most small businesses this is an advantage because not only is the 'end of March' an easier date to remember, you can effectively push five days' worth of income into the next tax year. And a deferral of tax is the next best thing to avoiding it altogether!

In some cases businesses that start up in the middle of the tax year prepare a complete 12 months of accounts from, say, 1 July 2007 to 30 June 2008.

It is possible to prepare a tax return on this basis but, quite frankly, it involves a lot more work.

It's far easier to have a short period from 1 July 2007 to 31 March 2008 and then use a financial year in sync with your tax year-end dates.

Whatever the Revenue and Customs may say in their television ads, tax is 'taxing' so keep it simple where you can!

Which Form?

There are now two different forms for self employment: the 'short' and the 'full'. The short form is only 2 pages long (SES in Customs and Revenue speak) and the full form (SEF) is 8 pages long. The two main criteria for using the short form are:

- Your total turnover for the year is under £64,000 (2007/8), or £5,333 per month if you have been trading for less than a year.
- You make your accounts up to the 5th April (or 31st March) each year

There are also several other reasons for not being able to use the short form mentioned in the guidance notes ('SESN'), which apply to only a few taxpayers. The biggest two groups of people unable to use the shorter version are probably those with a larger turnover, or those choosing to draw up accounts to dates other than the tax year end. In Chapters 11 and 12 I cover the short form in some detail and in Chapter 13 discuss the additional issues you need to consider with the full version.

Preparing the Information

By following the bookkeeping guidelines in this book, there should be no mad panic to get your records up to date when the time comes to complete your tax return.

The main things you need to ensure are that:

- You have included all sales invoices for work undertaken during the tax year.

- You have included all purchase invoices for expenses you have incurred.

- Your bank account reconciles with the information in your accounting spreadsheet.

- You have worked out how much stock you have on hand, and what it cost you to buy.

Accruals Accounting

The accounts I have been showing you how to complete are constructed on the *accruals* basis.

The accruals basis is used by most businesses. What counts under this system is when you make a sale or do a piece of work. The date you receive payment is not relevant.

For some sole traders, such as shopkeepers, there is no real distinction between the accrual basis and the cash basis. For other types of business it can be important. Some of the important issues are outlined later on to avoid confusing matters too much at this stage.

Chapter 11

Case Study 1
Turnover Under £30,000

To show you how to prepare your short self employment tax return let's bring back James and his book sales.

Last time we saw James he had just started his business. Now he's reached the end of March and his sales and expenses sheets are laid out below. To keep it simple I've ignored all the intervening transactions (represented by cross hatching in the figures below):

Sales

Figure 11.1 James's Sales: January 1ˢᵗ - March 31ˢᵗ

Week	Description	Amount	Title One	Title Two	Title Three
01/01/2008	eBay	1,000.00	250.00	150.00	600.00
08/01/2008	eBay	250.00	150.00	50.00	50.00
08/01/2008	Website	100.00	25.00	25.00	50.00
25/03/2008	eBay	500.00	150.00	50.00	300.00
Total		3,650.00	950.00	600.00	2,100.00

Expenses

Figure 11.2 James's Expenses: January 1ˢᵗ - March 31ˢᵗ

No.	Date	Payee	Description	Amount	Stationery	Paypal	eBay
1	05/01/2008	Staples	Office Supplies	59.50	59.50		
2	06/01/2008	PayPal	Transaction Fees	8.99		8.99	
3	08/01/2008	eBay	Seller's Fees	105.00			105.00
4	09/01/2008	PayPal	Transaction Fees	8.50		8.50	
28	31/03/2008	eBay	Seller's Fees	98.00			98.00
				-			
				541.20	81.50	66.70	393.00

I'm going to show you how to complete the self-employment pages of your tax return, using James's business as an example.

This document consists of just two pages in which you have to provide details of your business income and expenses.

Assuming you registered with Revenue and Customs when you started your sole trader business these extra tax return pages will be sent out to you automatically. Alternatively, you can download them from the HMRC website,

http://www.hmrc.gov.uk/forms/sa103s.pdf

In the pages below we'll take a closer look at each of the pages. It might be a good idea to go to the above web address and print out a copy now. There are only two pages after all and having them beside you while you read this chapter may make things a little easier.

Page SES1

Business Details

Illustrated is the first half of page SES1, the first of the self-employment pages. Your name goes at the top left of this form and your 'Tax reference' at top right. The tax reference is a 10-digit code, also known as your 'Unique Tax Reference' or UTR. This number should already be printed on the front left side of the first page of your tax return if you received one in the post. It usually also appears on any correspondence from Revenue and Customs.

If you have never registered as self employed, you may not have a record set up and this will prevent you from filing online. When you submit your first return a UTR number will be allocated. You will find the following boxes under the "Business Details" of the self-employment pages **SES1**

- **Box 1** asks for a description of the business. You should try to be as specific as possible. The form doesn't ask you for the trading name of the business, but I would suggest you add this too if you have one and there is space to do so.

- **Box 2** is your business postcode. If you work from home you can leave this blank as James has done.

- **Box 3** asks you to put a note in box 19 "Any other information" which can be found on page TR6 of the main return if any of the above details have changed. This is not relevant for James.

- **Box 4** asks a rather specific question about foster carers. If this applies to you please read the indicated guidance note.

- **Boxes 5 and 6** are for the start and end dates of trading. Box 5 is completed here with the date James started to trade – January 1st , when the first book contract was signed. Box 6 isn't relevant for James.

- **Box 7** shows the date the accounts are drawn up to. This is usually the same as the tax year. He started trading on January 1 2007 and, to keep things simple, chooses a tax year ending on March 31 2007.

56

Business Income

Business income - if your annual business turnover was below £64,000

8 Your turnover - *the takings, fees, sales or money earned by your business*	9 Any other business income not included in box 8 - *excluding Business Start-up allowance*
£ 3 6 5 0 . 0 0	£ . 0 0

There are only two boxes here. James simply transfers his total sales of £3,650 into box 8. There is no other income for box 9, but if there was sundry income excluded from his turnover he would enter this here.

Allowable Business Expenses

Allowable business expenses

Read page SESN 3 of the *notes* to see which expenses are allowable for tax purposes. If your annual turnover was below £30,000 you may just put your total expenses in box 19, rather than filling in the whole section.

10 Costs of goods bought for re-sale or goods used	15 Accountancy, legal and other professional fees
£ . 0 0	£ . 0 0
11 Car, van and travel expenses - *after private use proportion*	16 Interest and bank and credit card etc. financial charges
£ . 0 0	£ . 0 0
12 Wages, salaries and other staff costs	17 Telephone, fax, stationery and other office costs
£ . 0 0	£ . 0 0
13 Rent, rates, power and insurance costs	18 Other allowable business expenses - *client entertaining costs are not an allowable expense*
£ . 0 0	£ . 0 0
14 Repairs and renewals of property and equipment	19 Total allowable expenses - *total of boxes 10 to 18*
£ . 0 0	£ 5 4 2 . 0 0

Tax Return: Self-employment (short): Page SES 1

This section, still on page SES1 details business expenses.

If your turnover is under £30,000 you are able to put just your total expenses in box 19 rather than filling in the detailed boxes 10 to 18.

What the form doesn't make clear is that this is an *annualised* figure. In other words, if you've only been trading for three months your annualised turnover will be greater than your actual turnover. In other words, your annualised turnover may be more than £30,000 even if your actual turnover isn't.

James has been trading for only three months. To work out whether he has to itemise his expenses, he takes the £30,000 limit and divides by 12 months. This gives him a figure of £2,500 per month. He then multiplies this by the three months he has been in business, giving him a figure of £7,500. This is somewhat above his actual turnover of £3,650 and therefore James only has to provide his total expenses and doesn't have to split them into categories.

James therefore enters £542 in Box 19, being the total of his expenses for the period. You may notice that the shaded figure on the expenses spreadsheet above is £541.20 but the total in this box is £542. This is due to the rather odd way Revenue and Customs handles rounding. Expenses are always rounded up and turnover is rounded down.

Page SES2

That's page one finished and onto page two which should be a little easier.

Net Profit or Loss

There are two boxes in this section, 20 and 21. James has made a profit of £3,108, being the turnover of £3,650 in box 8 less the allowable expenses of £542 in box 19. This is entered as shown in box 20. Had James made a loss this would be entered in box 21.

Tax Allowances for Vehicles and Equipment (Capital Allowances)

Tax allowances for vehicles and equipment (capital allowances)

There are capital tax allowances for vehicles and equipment used in your business (you should not have included the cost of these in your business expenses). Read pages SESN 3 to SESN 6 of the notes and use the example and Working Sheets to work out your capital allowances.

22 Total capital allowances	23 Total balancing charges – where you have disposed of items for more than their value *read page SESN 4 of the notes*
£ · 0 0	£ · 0 0

The next section on page SES1 deals with capital allowances. These allow you to claim a tax deduction for various assets such as computers and furniture, which depreciate in value over time.

This section is not relevant to James, so is left blank for now. However, we will return to this important section in a more detailed example in Chapter 13.

Calculating Your Taxable Profits

Calculating your taxable profits

Your taxable profit may not be the same as your net profit. Read page SESN 7 of the *notes* to see if you need to make any adjustments and fill in the boxes which apply to arrive at your taxable profit for the year.

24 Goods or services for your own use – *read page SESN 7 of the notes*	26 Loss brought forward from earlier years set-off against this year's profits – up to the amount in box 25
£ · 0 0	£ · 0 0
25 Net business profit for tax purposes (box 20 or box 21 + box 23 + box 24 minus box 22)	27 Any other business income not included in boxes 8 or 9 – for example, Business Start-up Allowance
£ 3 1 0 8 · 0 0	£ · 0 0

Total taxable profits or net business loss

28 Total taxable profits from this business (box 25 + box 27 minus box 26)	29 Net business loss for tax purposes (if box 20 or box 21 + box 23 + box 24 minus box 22 is negative)
£ 3 1 0 8 · 0 0	£ · 0 0

James simply brings his taxable profit of £3,108 from box 20 down to box 25 and down again to box 28.

No further entries in this section are required for James as his affairs are simple. I cover the other boxes in the following chapter, including how to deal with losses.

And that, believe it or not, is the extent of James's self-employment pages. The only thing left is to make sure you have ticked question two on page TR2 of the main return to show you have enclosed the self-employment pages and indicated how many sets of self employment pages are enclosed (one in this instance).

As a form-filling exercise it is quite straightforward once you know how to draw up your records and where the numbers go.

Form filling aside, what we haven't looked at is one major issue – are all the expenses tax deductible? And, just as important, is there anything else that is deductible that we haven't yet recorded in our records? These sorts of questions are outside the scope of this book but are very important none the less.

Chapter 12

Case Study 2
Turnover from £30,000 to £64,000

Having warmed up with an easy example it's time to tackle something a little more involved. Step forward Emily and her art business. Business for Emily has been growing fast. Figures 12.1 and 12.2 show her sales and stock spreadsheets:

Figure 12.1 Emily's Sales Spreadsheet

Ref	Invoice Date	Customer	Artist	Amount	Paid Date	Cost	Gross Profit
INV001	01/01/2008	Mr A	Anna	1,000.00	08/01/2008	700.00	300.00
INV002	02/01/2008	Mr C	Paul	250.00	22/01/2008	100.00	150.00
INV003	05/01/2008	Mrs D	Peter	100.00	Bad	25.00	75.00
INV017	20/03/2008	Mr Y	Ali	500.00	25/03/2008	300.00	200.00
INV018	25/03/2008	Mrs Z	Kai	700.00	o/s	450.00	250.00
Total				12,150.00		9,500.00	2,650.00

Figure 12.2 Emily's Stock Spreadsheet

Date Purchased	Artist	Item Name	Purchase Price	Date Sold	Stock Value
01/12/2007	Anna	Flowers	700.00	01/01/2008	-
01/12/2007	Paul	Seascape	100.00	02/01/2008	-
01/12/2007	Peter	Calm	25.00	05/01/2008	-
01/12/2007	John	Face	400.00	22/02/2008	-
25/03/2008	Anna	Vase	500.00	Stock	500.00
	Total		10,000.00		500.00

An abridged version of her expenses spreadsheet is shown in Figure 12.3. (I have shaded out the descriptions and a number of the transactions so we just have a few lines as an example.)

Figure 12.3 Emily's Expenses Spreadsheet

No.	Total	Stock	Drawings	Shipping	Admin	Interest	Advert	Travel	Rent
1	300	300							
2	200						200		
3	50							50	
4	100								100
52	500.00	500.00							
-	-								
	17,978.00	10,000.00	5,000.00	100.00	75.00	- 12.00	575.00	240.00	2,000.00

Immediately we can see there is quite a bit more information to deal with, which means her tax return is going to be a little more complicated.

Page SES1

Business Details

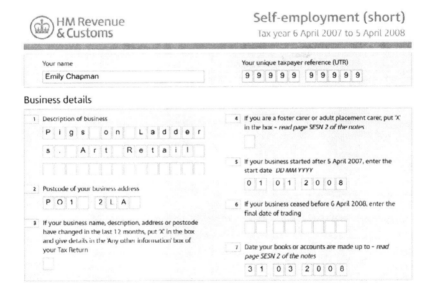

The first page of the self-employment pages is much the same as in the previous example, with Emily's business covering the same time periods as James. The main differences are that Emily has a trading name – 'Pigs on Ladders' – included in **box 1**, whereas

James traded in his own name, and Emily has an address that she trades from other than her home address. The post code for her business address is entered into box 2. The rest of the address isn't actually required.

Since her turnover is below £64,000 on an annualised basis (it's £12,150 over three months or £48,600 per annum), she is also eligible for the 'short' rather than the 'full' return which is covered in Chapter 13.

Business Income

Business income - if your annual business turnover was below £64,000

8 Your turnover – *the takings, fees, sales or money earned by your business*	9 Any other business income not included in box 8 – *excluding Business Start-up allowance*
£ 1 2 1 5 0 . 0 0	£ 1 2 . 0 0

Again this is fairly straightforward. Emily simply transfers her total sales of £12,150 into box 8.

Box 9 also applies this time. If you look at the expenses spreadsheet (Figure 12.3), there is a negative number '-12.00' in the 'Interest' column. Instead of having interest as an expense (for example on a business loan) Emily has earned interest and therefore has some extra income to report. She has included this in the box 9 figure.

The interest could equally as well be shown on box 1 on page TR3 of the main return and in fact if you have significant sums of interest (say more than about £50) I suggest you show it on page TR3 rather than here as you will benefit from any tax deducted by the bank which isn't taken into account if entered here in box 9.

Allowable Business Expenses

Allowable business expenses

Read page SESN 3 of the *notes* to see which expenses are allowable for tax purposes. If your annual turnover was below £30,000 you may just put your total expenses in box 19, rather than filling in the whole section.

10 Costs of goods bought for re-sale or goods used	£ 9 6 0 0 . 0 0		**15** Accountancy, legal and other professional fees	£ . 0 0
11 Car, van and travel expenses - *after private use proportion*	£ 2 1 5 . 0 0		**16** Interest and bank and credit card etc. financial charges	£ . 0 0
12 Wages, salaries and other staff costs	£ . 0 0		**17** Telephone, fax, stationery and other office costs	£ 7 5 . 0 0
13 Rent, rates, power and insurance costs	£ 2 0 0 0 . 0 0		**18** Other allowable business expenses - *client entertaining costs are not an allowable expense*	£ 6 7 5 . 0 0
14 Repairs and renewals of property and equipment	£ . 0 0		**19** Total allowable expenses - *total of boxes 10 to 18*	£ 1 2 5 6 5 . 0 0

Tax Return: Self-employment (short): Page SES 1

As Emily's turnover exceeds £30,000 on an annualised basis (it would be £48,600 as computed above if pro-rated over the whole year) Emily needs to fill in boxes 10 to 18 as well as box 19. This is essentially just a break down of the total figure.

If you want to know exactly what expenses go in each of the different categories, for example if you want to know what expenses you should enter in box 13 for Rent, rates, power and insurance costs, you'll find more detailed information in Appendix 2.

Box 10 Cost of sales

Let's kick off with the cost of sales, which are entered in **box 10**. For a retailer like Emily this is simply the purchase cost of all the stock she has sold during the year. If she was a manufacturer, for example if she painted the pictures herself, her cost of sales would be the cost of the raw materials: paint, canvas, picture frames, paint brushes etc.

The purchase cost of the paintings she has sold can be found on the sales spreadsheet (Figure 12.1), which lists how much Emily has paid for each of the paintings she sold. The total is £9,500.

We can also check the accuracy of this figure by looking at the stock spreadsheet, which shows the value of stock on hand at the end of the financial year and the total value of stock purchased:

	£
Total value of purchases	10,000
Less: value of stock at year-end	(500)
Cost of Goods Sold	9,500

This method shows the value of keeping slightly more records than you actually require, as you can double check the accuracy of your figures. In practice there could be other adjustments for things like damaged stock.

Thinking more widely about direct expenses, these are costs that vary directly in line with sales. It would not include rent, for example, because she would pay that even if she didn't sell any paintings.

It would include, for example, shipping costs or any commissions paid to other people who help her sell the paintings – in other words, costs that are directly related to selling the paintings. In Emily's case the amount spent on shipping is £100. The cost of shipping goods both to the end customer and for stock arriving at your shop is a "cost of sale" and included in this box.

Emily therefore enters into box 10 £9,600, comprising £9,500 for the stock sold, plus £100 for sending it out to customers.

Box 11 Car, van and travel expenses

This box includes travel and subsistence and business travel. In Emily's case the £240 includes bed and breakfast expenses, a train fare incurred meeting a supplier plus a £25 parking fine.

This parking fine is unfortunately not allowable for tax purposes. The £25 disallowable item is deducted before the entry of £215 you can see in box 11.

	£
Total travel expenses per fig 12.3	240
Less Disallowable parking fine	(25)
Allowable amount in box 11	215

If Emily used her car for business purposes the amounts would be entered here. For businesses under the VAT threshold there is the option of either:

- Claiming a share of the actual costs of the vehicle in proportion to the business and private usage, or
- Claiming mileage at a rate of 40p per business mile for the first 10,000 miles and 25p thereafter.

Which method is more beneficial to you will depend on your circumstances. It's worth noting that if you are a sole trader business with a turnover over the VAT threshold you will need to use the 'full cost' method. This is quite complicated and I recommend reading the guidance notes that come with your self assessment return if you plan to tackle this yourself. A proportion of the actual cost of the vehicle will be entered into box 22, "capital allowances" with the running costs entered in box 11.

Box 12 Wages, salaries and other staff costs

Emily doesn't have any employees, so **box 12** is left blank. If she did have employees she would put all the wages, employee benefits, national insurance contributions, recruitment agency fees and other staff-related costs in this box. This box won't contain her own national insurance contributions as these are not tax deductible.

You should note that 'drawings' (money taken out of the business by Emily for her personal use) are not included as an employee expense. Sole traders are not employees of their own businesses and cannot pay themselves a salary.

Instead they take drawings that are withdrawals of profit from the business. Because profits are calculated after deducting all expenses the drawings themselves are not a business expense.

Box 13 Rent, rates, power and insurance costs

Emily has paid £2,000 in rent and this goes into **box 13**. In practice she would also have other premises costs such as business rates, electricity and gas, and insurance premiums. These would all go in box 13.

Box 14 Repairs and renewals of property and equipment

This would include repairs she has to make to her business premises or any equipment she uses in the business. Again in this example this box is left blank for Emily.

Box 15 Accountancy, legal and other professional fees

Legal and professional costs, would be used for fees such as using a solicitor to draw up terms and conditions or accountancy fees for helping with your returns.

Box 16 Interest and bank and credit card etc. financial charges

This is for interest paid, such as on an overdraft or bank loan and other finance charges. You would also include related fees such as bank charges and overdraft fees you may incur. Fortunately Emily doesn't have any of these costs.

Box 17 Telephone, fax, stationery and other office costs

This is for general administrative expenses such as stationery and other office expenses. Emily has £75 to include here.

Box 18 Other allowable business expenses

This is the 'catch all' box for anything not entered into boxes 10 to 17. For Emily this includes £575 for advertising she has incurred promoting her business, mainly some flyers and some printed adverts in magazines.

There is also £100 for bad debts. This represents the unpaid invoice INV003 to Mrs D shown on figure 12.1. We know Mrs D is in serious financial difficulties (she has been declared bankrupt) and there is very little chance of this debt being paid.

We can therefore safely 'write off' the debt. This is different to the outstanding INV018 from Mrs Z, which we expect to be paid in a few days.

Box 19 Total Allowable expenses

This is simply the total of boxes 10 to 18. We will see below in 'final checks' how to ensure that this is actually the correct figure!

Using Your Spreadsheets

All of the above expense information was extracted with relative ease from the expenses spreadsheet in Figure 12.3.

In practice, what often happens is that you will have many more expense categories in your spreadsheet than there are on the tax return. This means several categories will have to be added together.

For example, you may list your phone bills and stationery separately, but they would both go under the "telephone, fax, stationery and other office costs" heading.

The trick is to always have too many and not too few categories. There is nothing worse than having to split, say, your motor expenses from your other travel and subsistence retrospectively.

In practice, it's worth making a note in your bookkeeping records to show in which tax return box number each expense category has been included. This will provide an 'audit trail' if HMRC ever enquires into your return and you need to work out what you did 2 or 3 years previously.

SES2

Onto the second page of the return.

Net Profit or Loss

Net profit or loss

20 Net profit - *if your business income is more than your expenses (box 8 + box 9 minus box 19)*

£ . 0 0

21 Or, net loss - *if your expenses exceed your business income (box 8 + box 9 minus box 19 is negative)*

£ 4 0 3 . 0 0

To calculate the net profit or loss we take the total incomes (boxes 8 and 9) and deduct the total expenses (box 19) as follows:

Sales Income + Other Income − Total Expenses = Net Profit or Loss

Boxes 8 + 9 − 19 = Box 20 or Box 21

£12,150 + £12 − £12,565 = − £403

Had Emily made a profit, this would be entered into box 20 as in the example of James above. As it is a loss it goes into box 21.

Tax Allowances for Vehicles and Equipment (Capital Allowances)

This section is not relevant to Emily, but is covered in the following chapter.

Calculating Your Taxable Profits

Calculating your taxable profits

Your taxable profit may not be the same as your net profit. Read page SESN 7 of the *notes* to see if you need to make any adjustments and fill in the boxes which apply to arrive at your taxable profit for the year.

24 Goods or services for your own use - *read page SESN 7 of the notes*	26 Loss brought forward from earlier years set-off against this year's profits - *up to the amount in box 25*
£ 2 0 0 . 0 0	£ . 0 0
25 Net business profit for tax purposes (box 20 or box 21 + box 23 + box 24 minus box 22)	27 Any other business income not included in boxes 8 or 9 - *for example, Business Start up Allowance*
£ . 0 0	£ . 0 0

Total taxable profits or net business loss

28 Total taxable profits from this business (box 25 + box 27 minus box 26)	29 Net business loss for tax purposes (if box 20 or box 21 + box 23 + box 24 minus box 22 is negative)
£ . 0 0	£ 2 0 3 . 0 0

This section works out any further adjustments to the taxable income.

Box 24 is used where a sole trader takes goods for their own use. Emily has taken goods with a resale value of £200 and used them at home, and therefore has entered £200 in box 24. You should note that is actually the normal *sales price* and not the purchase price that is used when adjusting for goods or services for your own use. This follows a recent court case and ruling. Historically the purchase price of the goods was used.

Box 25 would show the taxable profit if Emily had made one. However, in this example even after the adjustment for goods for personal use Emily has still got a taxable loss of £203.

Box 26 is where losses bought forward from earlier years are entered. As Emily is in her first year there is no entry here but as her losses will be carried forward to the following year, she will have an entry in this box next time around.

Box 27 is another 'catch all' box aimed at picking up any other income not already entered.

Box 28 would again show the taxable profit taken from box 25, as adjusted for any entries in boxes 26 and 27.

Box 29 is used when there is a taxable loss. In Emily's case this is £204.

$$box\ 21 + box\ 24 = box\ 29$$

$$£\text{-}403 + £200 = \text{-}£203$$

Losses, Class 4 NICs and Deductions

Losses, Class 4 NICs and deductions

If you have made a loss for tax purposes (box 29), read page SESN 7 of the *notes* and fill in boxes 30 to 32 as appropriate

30 Loss from this tax year set-off against other income for 2007-08	33 If you are exempt from paying Class 4 NICs, put 'X' in the box – *read page SESN 8 of the notes*
£ . 0 0	☐
31 Loss to be carried back to previous year(s) and set-off against income (or capital gains)	34 If you have been given a 2007-08 Class 4 NICs deferment certificate, put 'X' in the box – *read page SESN 8 of the notes*
£ . 0 0	☐
32 Total loss to carry forward after all other set-offs – *including unused losses brought forward*	35 Deductions on payment and deduction statements from contractors – *construction industry subcontractors only*
£ 2 0 3 . 0 0	£ . 0 0

Tax Return: Self-employment (short): Page SES 2

Boxes 30 to 32 are concerned with the use of any losses as a sole trader.

The basic theory is that you can offset trading losses against certain other income in the current year, for example a salary if you have one (**box 30**). This may get you immediate tax relief, in other words, real money back from the taxman!

You can carry a loss back to the previous tax year if you had a profit then (**box 31**), or if you have no profits in the prior year and nothing to offset it against in the current year, you can carry the loss forward to a future period (**box 32**).

The tax treatment of losses can get quite complicated. If you have one you should think about getting some help from an accountant to ensure you make the most of it.

In Emily's case, she has chosen to carry her losses forward to the next tax year (box 32) because she doesn't have any other PAYE income in the current period to offset the loss against and obtain a tax refund.

In the following year's tax return this £203 will appear in box 26

Box 33 exemption from Class 4 National insurance may be ticked if you are exempt. This applies broadly to young entrepreneurs under 16, and those at the other end of the scale who are still going past the official retirement age of 65 from men and 60 for women.

Box 34 National insurance deferment is somewhat different. This may apply in some cases where you already pay enough national insurance via your employment and you are a higher-rate taxpayer. If you are a higher-rate taxpayer you will need to apply separately for this deferment.

Box 35 is relevant to subcontractors in the construction industry scheme (CIS scheme) who have tax deducted from their wages before they are paid. The value of the tax deducted goes in this box.

Further initial guidance is available within the general help sheet "Self-employment (short) notes" which is posted to you with the paper copy of your tax return or is available to download from the HMRC website:

http://www.hmrc.gov.uk/worksheets/sa103s-notes.pdf

Final Checks

Once you have got all the numbers on to your tax return it makes a lot of sense to refer back to the source documents and check that everything stacks up and you haven't left anything out.

We originally had:

	£
Sales	*12,150*
Less total expenses	*(17,978)*
Unadjusted loss	*(5,828)*
Add back stock	*500*
Add back drawings	*5,000*
Add back parking fine	*25*
Add back stock for own use	*200*
Less bad debts	*(100)*
Net loss	*(203)*

The net loss calculated this way is, thankfully, the same as that appearing on the tax return in box 29.

If you are doing your own return it is well worth persevering with this sort of check to ensure you have got all the numbers into your return and added everything up correctly.

I know this has got a lot more complicated than the example of James, but it does demonstrate that things get a lot trickier once you throw in a few real-life issues and some adjustments are required.

Chapter 13

Further Self-Assessment Issues

This section covers some more advanced topics you'll need to understand to complete your own tax return.

Accruals and Prepayments

It's important to understand the basic accounting conventions of matching income and expenditure to the period in which they relate.

Typically, if you undertake long-term projects you may be in the middle of several jobs at the end of the year. In this instance you are obliged (under accruals accounting conventions) to estimate how much of the project has been completed, and therefore how much money you have earned but not billed.

Example

Richard designs websites. He has already sent out invoices totalling £20,000 and has three projects ongoing:

- *He is half way through a £5,000 web development project for Andrew, having billed £1,000.*

- *He has billed £500 towards a £2,000 site for Mary but has barely started the project.*

- *He has billed Paul for £2,000. Only £1,800 has been paid as there is a three-month retention period.*

For Andrew's project he has effectively earned £2,500 (i.e. half) and billed £1,000 and therefore needs to add £1,500 to his sales.

For Mary's project he has billed in advance and needs to deduct £500 as he hasn't actually done anything yet.

For Paul's project the site is complete and the £2,000 invoice has been sent out. Only if the site wasn't properly finished would there be any adjustment here.

So the total income is:

	£
Sales per spreadsheet	20,000
Accrual for Andrew	1,500
Less prepayment Mary	(500)
Total income	21,000

In the following year Andrew must remember to take off the £1,500 current year accrual from his income or he will be double counting his income.

This is often when people get confused when doing their own accounts. So if you need to make this sort of adjustment it may be worth getting help.

A similar principle applies to your expenses. For example, Emily in the previous example paid out £2,000 in rent. If this was paid out on March 1, for the three months March to May, only one-third (£667) would be tax deductible in the tax year to the end of March. The remaining £1,333 would have to be claimed in the following year.

Capital Allowances

To keep matters as simple as possible in the above examples, I skirted around the capital allowances section on page SES2. In practice most businesses are entitled to claim these allowances.

To understand the point of these, we have to look at the difference between 'revenue expenses' and 'capital expenses'. In short, a revenue expense is spending on something that is 'used up' quickly, for example, a meal or a train ticket.

A capital expense is something that will last longer than a year, for example a car, computer or building. Furthermore, capital items are normally substantial items rather than low-value items. For example, you wouldn't treat the purchase of a wastebasket as a capital expense, even if you get 20 years' life out of it.

The reason we have capital allowances is so that the cost of certain items can be spread over a number of years, rather than taking the whole cost as a tax deduction in year one.

You should note that there is no hard and fast cut off point where expenses cease being revenue and become capital. As a rule of thumb, if you use the item for less than 18 months or it costs less than £100, most tax inspectors seem to be happy with treating the item as a revenue expense. This means the total cost is tax deductible in the year of purchase.

That's if you're a sole trader. Larger businesses would generally not capitalize anything under £1,000.

Let's return to James and assume that, to run his business, he bought a laptop for £2,000.

The capital allowance computation is as follows:

Purchase	*£2,000*
First Year Allowance @ 50%	*(£1,000)*
Written-down value carried forward	*£1,000*

With effect from April 6 2007, sole traders enjoy a 50% first-year allowance on most assets.

It's important to point out that you are entitled to the full 50% even if you only buy the asset on the last day of the tax year. James is entitled to £1,000 of capital allowances, which means his taxable profits are reduced by £1,000.

His claim is shown on the revised Page SES2 (Figure 13.1) below:

Figure 13.1 Claiming Capital Allowances

Net profit or loss

20 Net profit - *if your business income is more than your expenses (box 8 + box 9 minus box 19)*	21 Or, net loss - *if your expenses exceed your business income (box 8 + box 9 minus box 19 is negative)*
£ 3 1 0 8 . 0 0	£ . 0 0

Tax allowances for vehicles and equipment (capital allowances)

There are capital tax allowances for vehicles and equipment used in your business (you should not have included the cost of these in your business expenses). Read pages SESN 3 to SESN 6 of the *notes* and use the example and Working Sheets to work out your capital allowances.

22 Total capital allowances	23 Total balancing charges - where you have disposed of items for more than their value - *read page SESN 4 of the notes*
£ 1 0 0 0 . 0 0	£ . 0 0

Calculating your taxable profits

Your taxable profit may not be the same as your net profit. Read page SESN 7 of the *notes* to see if you need to make any adjustments and fill in the boxes which apply to arrive at your taxable profit for the year.

24 Goods or services for your own use - *read page SESN 7 of the notes*	26 Loss brought forward from earlier years set-off against this year's profits *up to the amount in box 25*
£ . 0 0	£ . 0 0
25 Net business profit for tax purposes (box 20 or box 21 + box 23 + box 24 minus box 22)	27 Any other business income not included in boxes 8 or 9 *for example, Business Start up Allowance*
£ 2 1 0 8 . 0 0	£ . 0 0

Box 22 records the capital allowance of £1,000. This is then deducted from the net profit in box 20 to give the taxable profit in box 25 of £2,108.

In the second year a 'normal' 25% allowance is available. This rate is applicable to most 'Plant and Machinery' after the first year.

Bought forward value	*£1,000*
25% allowance in year two	*(£250)*
Written-down value carried forward	*£750*

Let's assume that in the third year James purchases a new laptop and receives £200 for the old one.

What happens now is that a 'balancing allowance' is calculated, being the difference between the written-down value and the amount received for the laptop.

Written-down value carried forward　　£750
Part exchange value　　　　　　　　　(£200)
Balancing allowance　　　　　　　　　£550

The above summary is a very basic guide to capital allowances, and will just about see you through if you simply have a computer and a few sundry items.

Capital allowances can, however, be extremely complex. There are all sorts of special rules and rates. For example, I haven't covered the rules about cars and assets that have shared personal and business usage.

There are also different rates for different assets, so unless you have very simple affairs you may need to seek further advice. A good place to start is Revenue and Customs' self-employment (full) notes on page SEFN10. The link for this is given in the next section.

You may like to note that for tax periods starting April 2008 (tax returns for the period 2008/9 onwards) a different regime will be in place. There will be a 100% capital allowance (the full cost is allowable in the first year) for up to £50,000 of capital spending. There will be a lower 20% writing down allowance and several other changes too.

Self Employment (Full)

In the preceding chapters we have concentrated on the 'short' form which is applicable broadly speaking if your turnover is under £64,000 and your accounting periods align to the tax year.

For those of you with a larger business you unfortunately need the more detailed form 'Self-employment (full)' (SEF). The good news is this is just more of the same with different box numbers. I take you through the main features to look out for on the full return below.

You can download a copy of the form from the HMRC website:

http://www.hmrc.gov.uk/forms/sa103f.pdf

The accompanying help sheet can be found here:

http://www.hmrc.gov.uk/worksheets/sa103f-notes.pdf

Let's take a closer look at the various sections:

SEF1

Business details. This is largely the same as before with a few more details required, such as the name of your business.

Other information. Only box 10 "if you accounting date has changed permanently" is likely to apply to most small businesses.

Business income. This is identical to the short return as discussed in the earlier chapters.

SEF2

Business expenses. At first glance this looks a lot more detailed but in reality there are just a few more categories of expenses listed in the left hand column, and any disallowable expenses are listed in the right hand column. In practice you can simply deduct the disallowable expenses and include the net figure in the left hand column if that's easier.

You should note that if you are used to the old tax form in use for tax years up to 2006/7, the allowable/disallowable columns are now listed the other way around – disallowed items were previously shown on the left so be careful if you are used to the old form!

SEF3

Net profit or loss. This is the same as the short return.

Tax allowances for vehicles and equipment (capital allowances). This looks rather confusing at first glance, but the main boxes are box 48 if you have a company car and box 49 for general capital allowances. The total allowances go in box 55. The other boxes are likely to apply to only a minority of businesses.

Calculating your taxable profit or loss. This is where things start to get rather more complex, and this section continues onto page SEF4. The 'vanilla' entry is simply box 62 (net profit), and box 64 and 65 showing your "basis period" (in other words, the dates to which you have drawn up the accounts). If you think any other boxes apply you probably need to get some professional help as a lot of the concepts here are quite complex, including where your accounts are drawn up to a different date than the tax year as you will have to fiddle about with overlap relief (boxes 66 to 68).

SEF4

Losses. Box 75 is equivalent to box 29 on the short form, i.e. the total losses computed. Boxes 76, 77 and 78 are just the same as boxes 30, 31 and 32 discussed in the preceding chapter.

Deductions and tax taken off. Include in box 79 any CIS deductions you have suffered if you are in the CIS scheme. Put any other tax not included elsewhere in box 80. This will probably be bank interest if you have included your gross interest in box 15, rather than including it on page TR3 of the main tax return.

SEF5

Balance sheet. This section is where you put details of your business balance sheet. The important point to make here is that this page is completely voluntary! That is to say Revenue and Customs does not insist that you complete it.

There is therefore little to be gained by putting this information together.

Creating a balance sheet requires a good understanding of double entry bookkeeping and is beyond most small business owners. It's an 'optional extra' that your accountant may provide for your own management purposes but is not something you need to be concerned about when completing your tax return.

Class 4 National Insurance contributions. If you are exempt or deferring your NI then you would tick boxes 98 and 99 respectively. For more details see the example of Emily above. Box 100 is unlikely to apply to you.

SEF5

Any other information. This can be used to give additional information where directed to do so elsewhere on the form.

The only practical use of this is to provide additional explanations to HMRC where you have unusual entries, for example a very large entry in any of the boxes. For example, if Emily had taken £10,000 of goods for private use in box 24, rather than £200, this would be quite unusual given her turnover of £12,150 and may spark questions about the accuracy of the return. The Revenue and Customs computers use statistical analysis to spot oddities for further investigation, so it helps to have a ready explanation.

Chapter 14

General Self-Assessment Tips

- Don't leave your tax return until the last minute. If you are completing it yourself you will almost certainly find things you need to check, which could take some time.

- Revenue and Customs publishes a number of guides to help you complete your tax return. They aren't very practical but do help you with specific boxes. Have a look at the *Self-employment (short) notes*

  www.hmrc.gov.uk/worksheets/sa103s-notes.pdf

  and *Self-employment (full) notes*:

  www.hmrc.gov.uk/worksheets/sa103f-notes.pdf

  Also look at help sheets IR220 through to IR326, some of which deal with various specific trades and situations:

  www.hmrc.gov.uk/selfemployed/fagsa103.shtml

- Complete your return online. As long as you don't leave it until January, when the whole system is painfully slow, the online filing for self-assessment is really quite good. Not only does it add up a lot of the boxes for you, it now directs you to the parts of the return you must complete, with relevant questions and checks to see if you have made any obvious errors.

  Filling in your tax return online also cuts out the risk of Revenue and Customs making keying errors when manually processing your paper return.

There is a small initial delay because you need to register for this service in advance and security codes are sent out to you. But once registered you can ensure that your return is submitted on time and find out much faster what you owe or are owed.

- Paper forms should now be submitted by the end of October. Despite this, HMRC have stated fines will not be levied so long as the form is returned and the correct tax is paid by 31 January. If you are completing your return after the end of October, in order to be able to compute the amount of tax due you will realistically need to prepare your return using the Revenue and Customs website or 3rd party software in any case. If you are unable to do this, overestimate the amount of tax due and pay this over to avoid a fine. You will get back the overpayment in due course.

- If you really don't know what you are doing, get some proper help. It really is a case of 'garbage in, garbage out'. It doesn't matter how beautifully you fill in the forms, if the numbers are wrong you may end up paying too much or too little tax.

With the demise of the local tax office and the growth of the call centre, the quality of help available from Revenue and Customs can vary considerably. So always call twice to ensure that you get the same answer. Daft though it may seem, things really can be this hit and miss. For VAT enquiries a transcript of the conversation is made and put on your file. If it transpires that you have been misled you will tend to get an apology rather than a fine. Unfortunately no such niceties occur with self assessment unless you have an answer in writing.

Section 5

Accounting for Limited Companies

Chapter 15

The Basics

So far this guide has looked at the accounting and tax treatment of sole trader businesses only. There are, however, two main ways to trade in the UK: as a sole trader/partnership or through a limited company.

The main reason to trade as a sole trader is simplicity both in terms of set up and record keeping. The main reasons to trade as a limited company are added credibility, limitation of liability and some tax advantages.

Given that many readers may at some point wish to run their business through a company, it's useful to outline the main issues. In particular, a limited company has additional reporting requirements and also requires a fundamental improvement in the quality of your accounting records.

In the first bookkeeping section we covered accounting controls and reconciliation of your business bank account. As a sole trader, any overlap between your personal money and the money of the business can be glossed over to a certain extent when completing your self-assessment tax return.

With a limited company no such short-cut can be made as the limited company and the owner/director are separate legal entities. Transactions between a company and its directors have important tax implications and directors have certain statutory legal obligations.

Chapter 16

How to Benefit from a Director's Loan Account

Going back to our very basic spreadsheets we had three tabs:

1. Sales
2. Expenses
3. Bank Account

We now add a fourth:

4. The Director's Loan Account

The purpose of the director's loan account is to track all payments between a director and the company. There are several reasons these transactions may occur.

Payments Due from Company to Director	Payments Due from Director to Company
Initial or additional capital injected into the business by the director.	Cash sums taken out of the company for personal use.
Business expenses incurred personally by the director and not reimbursed.	Sales receipts received into personal bank account or in cash.
Salaries or bonus awarded but not paid.	Personal items paid for with company money.
Dividends awarded but not paid.	

The following spreadsheet (Figure 16.1) shows an example loan account:

Figure 16.1 Example Loan Account

			Paid	Due To Director		Balance
			£	£		£
01/01/2008	Start up funding		-	1,000.00		1,000.00
02/02/2008	Expenses		-	154.75		1,154.75
01/03/2008	Salary March		300.00	300.00		1,154.75
01/04/2008	Salary April		300.00	300.00		1,154.75
01/05/2008	Salary May		-	300.00		1,454.75
25/05/2008	Payment Made		6,000.00	-		- 4,545.25
01/06/2008	Salary June		-	300.00		- 4,245.25
15/06/2008	Interim Dividend		-	5,000.00		754.75

- An initial loan of £1,000 was made to the company on the 1st of January as a start-up fund.

- A personal expense claim of £154.75 was submitted on 2nd of February, but has not been paid by the company.

- The March and April salaries were paid out immediately.

- The May salary was awarded but not paid over.

- On the 25th May a large payment of £6,000 was made to the director, but because not all the salaries had been taken and the initial loan of £1,000 was made, the account was overdrawn by only £4,545.25

- The June salary was awarded but not paid over.

- The dividend declared on the 15th June put the account back 'in the black'.

You should note that you could dispense with the transactions on 1 March and 1 April when the salary was paid out in full. I personally prefer to keep a full record of all transactions between the director and the company.

The loan account spreadsheet doesn't exist in isolation from the other tabs on your spreadsheet. Each of these transactions will also have an entry on the other sheets.

For example the start-up funding of £1,000 will appear on the banking page as a deposit into the business bank account. Similarly the expenses and salaries will all appear on the expenses spreadsheet.

It is worth noting that we tend to use the word 'expenses' to mean two slightly different things, both business expenses incurred by the business and expenses incurred by the individual director on behalf of the business.

Fundamentally every transaction will have a second entry – this is the basis of double-entry bookkeeping, which, although outside the scope of the guide, is what you are actually doing in a small way.

When reconciling your bank account you will now have all three pages to contend with – the balance in the bank will be equal to all your sales, less all your expenses less the movements on the director's loan account after accounting for unpaid invoices.

I won't go into much more detail about taking money out of a limited company, but fundamentally this account becomes the buffer between you and the company. If you keep accurate records you can use the loan account to minimise the amounts you take in taxable salary and dividends.

What tends to happen in practice is that a dividend is formally declared every three to six months. However, instead of being paid it is left on the director's loan account (as per the transaction above on 15 June) and then drawn down over the next few months, as funds are required.

There is also the ability to overdraw the Director's Loan Account by up to £5,000 without penalty so long as the account is repaid within nine months of your company year-end. You really need to sit down with your accountant to go through the correct plan for your business, as payments to directors can become quite complex.

Chapter 17

How to Claim Back Money from Your Company

Practical Aspects

In running a small limited company the aim should be to keep your affairs as simple as possible – the fewer adjusting transactions between you and the company the better. By following these four simple steps you can make your life a lot simpler:

- All sales income should be credited to the company bank account.

- No personal expenditures should be made with company money.

- Where you incur business costs with personal money (e.g, purchase items on your credit card or business mileage) a formal expense claim should be submitted.

- Do not overdraw your director's loan account by more than £5,000 at any time.

Submission of an Expense Claim

As noted above one of the important aspects of managing a limited company is controlling transactions between the directors and the company. Although you should try to get the company to pay for as many expenses as possible, you will inevitably make some business purchases with personal money.

In order to keep this as simple and as structured as possible you should put in place a simple expense claim process to deal with these transactions on a weekly or monthly basis. There is no set format you need to follow and at its most simple you can just list the expenses on a sheet of A4, staple the receipts to the back of it and treat the claim just like an invoice from a supplier.

At a slightly more sophisticated level you could treat expense claims just like a mini set of accounts, with separate columns for different types of expenses.

Let's look at an example. Let's say Richard runs a small limited company and has the following claim for expenses he has incurred personally (Figure 17.1)

Figure 17.1 Personal Expense Claim

No.	Date	Payee	Purpose	Amount	Subsis	Travel	Accom	Insurance
1	06/01/2008	Paul's Café	Lunch	5.25	5.25			
2	06/01/2008	Ariva	Train to meeting	39.50		39.50		
3	07/01/2008	Trusthouse Forte	Meeting AB&Co	110.00			110.00	
				-				
				-				
				154.75	5.25	39.50	110.00	0

Richard had a meeting with AB & Co on 6 January, resulting in a claim for lunch, a rail ticket and overnight accommodation. The total claim is £154.75. With expenses claims, it is generally advisable to state the 'purpose' of the claim to show it was a legitimate business expense. There are lots of odd rules about what you can and can't claim but generally if you genuinely incur an expense 100% for business reasons, it will be deductible.

Richard staples his invoices to the back of his claim, so he has proof of the expenses to hand.

In terms of his main bookkeeping records, Figure 17.2 shows how the entry would look as one line on his business expenses spreadsheet.

Figure 17.2 Business Expenses Spreadsheet

No.	Date	Payee	Description	Amount	Subsis	Travel	Accom	Insurance
856	02/02/2008	Richard	Jan Expenses	154.75	5.25	39.50	110.00	
				-				
				-				
				154.75	5.25	39.50	110.00	0

As you can see, we don't simply have a separate analysis column for 'personally incurred expenses', and drop the total in. Instead we split the personal expenses into the different categories.

In terms of his director's loan account, if the full amount is not paid out, then this would appear as an increase in the director's loan account.

Note that if Richard had been VAT registered we would need to know what expenses included VAT and therefore what was reclaimable by the business. For the avoidance of doubt VAT incurred by a director on behalf of a business can be reclaimed on the company VAT return in the normal way so long as proper records are kept.

Reclaiming Business Mileage

Given the high tax on company-owned vehicles, company car ownership is becoming quite rare in small businesses. Claims for business mileage undertaken in personal vehicles are therefore increasingly common.

Generally business mileage can be claimed on journeys made for business purposes in your own car. The mileage you can claim is the *lesser* of:

- The distance from your normal place of work to your destination, or

- The distance from your start point (for example, your home) to your destination.

Where a business is based at home, your home will be classified as your normal place of work. In other words, all mileage for business purposes can be claimed.

Where business mileage is claimed, it is a requirement that each journey is listed with the following information: the date, the start point, the destination and the purpose of the visit. An example is contained in figure 17.3.

Figure 17.3 Business Mileage Log

Date	From	To	Purpose	Miles	Cost
25/3/2008	Office	Manchester	Visit Mr A Consultation	315	£126.00
26/3/2008	Office	Ipswich	Acorn Ltd, repair	25	£10.00
			Total	340	£136.00

The rates under the 'Fixed Profit Car Scheme' are 40p per mile for the first 10,000 business miles travelled during the tax year, and 25p thereafter.

This is why the total cost in the above spreadsheet is £136: 340 miles x 40p.

If you do a lot of business mileage it is therefore necessary to keep a running total (measured on a tax year basis) so you know at what point you pass the 10,000-mile threshold.

The total amount of £136 would be added to the basic expense claim as above and processed the same way.

Care should be taken to ensure that actual distances are used and not rough estimates. If in doubt use something like the RAC or AA route planner to check distances:

www.rac.co.uk/web/routeplanner

I often find it is easier to enter a list of postcodes into a route planner than mess around with a notepad in the car.

Tax Tip

Although VAT cannot be claimed on the full 40p, there is a VAT reclaim available for a portion that is notionally allocated to fuel. There are published rates of the 'fuel' element depending on the size of the car engine, which works out to a couple of pence per mile. If you do a lot of mileage (and it's not worthwhile if you only do a few thousand) it may be worth following up this point.

Chapter 18

Limited Company Summary

The previous section has given you a brief overview of some of the extra record keeping requirements for companies. If you endeavour to keep your business and your personal finances as separate as possible you shouldn't run into too many problems with your bookkeeping.

Finally, I'm leaving this section with a short plea – if you are running a limited company please get yourself an accountant at the earliest opportunity. This isn't a desperate measure to drum up business for my profession. It comes from frustration at seeing decent hardworking people getting very stressed and spending a lot of time trying to deal with and submit their own limited company accounts – often with expensive consequences in terms of late filing fees and poor practices.

Fundamentally, if your business is big enough to have incorporated, it should be big enough to allow for a few hundred pounds in professional fees to get things sorted out properly. In most cases the fees are easily recovered once all the proper tax planning is put in place to utilise the tax breaks available to you.

Section 6

Everything You Need to Know About VAT

Chapter 19

Basic Bookkeeping with VAT

In the pages that follow we'll look at how to practically set out your records if you need to account for VAT and how to complete your quarterly VAT return.

This section builds on the earlier bookkeeping chapters. If you are diving straight in here, it may be helpful to read through the earlier sections to familiarise yourself with the spreadsheet formats I use in the examples.

Sales Spreadsheet

Let's kick off with a simple example of sales income for a service business. Here's how the information is recorded on the sales spreadsheet (Figure 19.1)

Figure 19.1 Sales Spreadsheet Including VAT

Ref	Description	Date	Net	VAT	Gross	Date Paid
INV001	Mr A	01/01/2008	1,000.00	175.00	1,175.00	23/01/2008
INV002	Mr C	02/01/2008	250.00	43.75	293.75	
Total			1,250.00	218.75	1,468.75	

- 'Ref' is the sequential and unique invoice number
- 'Description' is the client's name and perhaps the work completed
- 'Date' is the invoice date
- 'Net' is the pre-VAT cost
- 'VAT' is the VAT charge
- 'Gross' is the VAT-inclusive figure billed to the client
- 'Date paid' the date the payment cleared in the business bank account

This is identical to the very first example given in Chapter 1, except that the totals are split into Net, VAT and Gross.

96

Furthermore, a 'Date Paid' column has been added, the use of which will become apparent shortly when we look at preparing the VAT return.

Net vs Gross

It is helpful at this point to remind yourself what net and gross mean in practical terms.

- 'Net' is the amount that you actually earn – this is the number that will appear in your accounts as turnover.

- 'VAT' is the amount of tax that you will eventually pay over to HM Revenue and Customs.

- 'Gross' is the total amount of the invoice you are sending out, and the amount of actual money you are going to be paid by your customer.

Excel Tip - Make the Formulas do the Hard Work

When using spreadsheets, it makes a lot of sense to calculate the VAT due using a formula as this will save a lot of pointless data entry.

Emily, who sells art to the general public, may sell an item for £200 inclusive of VAT. She will then need to work out the VAT from this total gross sales price.

Someone else selling professional services will tend to quote a fee such as £100 + VAT.

Emily will enter the £200 in the gross column on her spreadsheet and set up two formulas:

- Net = Gross / 1.175
- VAT = Gross – Net

Someone selling professional services will enter the £100 in the net column and set up two similar formulas:

- VAT = Net * 0.175
- Gross = Net + VAT

Taxcafe has a useful VAT calculator that does both these calculations for you. It is available free from:

www.taxcafe.co.uk/vatcalc

Expenses Spreadsheet

Now we have dealt with the income, the expenses should be relatively straightforward. The basic layout below (Figure 19.2) is much the same as in the original example in Chapter 1:

Figure 19.2 Expenses Spreadsheet Including VAT

No.	Date	Payee	Description	Gross	VAT	Net	Stationery	Books	Drawings
1	05/01/2008	Staples	Office Supplies	59.50	8.86	50.64	50.64		
2	06/01/2008	Taxcafe	Books	24.95	-	24.95		24.95	
3	22/01/2008	Self	Drawings	105.00	-	105.00			105.00
				189.45	8.86	180.59	50.64	24.95	105.00

- 'Net' is the pre-VAT cost
- 'VAT' is the VAT charge
- 'Gross' is the VAT-inclusive figure that you physically pay

You should note one important item here – the analysis columns are based on the *net* of VAT figures, rather than the gross figures. This is important because when it comes to drawing up your accounts it is these after-VAT figures we are interested in.

Unfortunately, it's common for accountants to have to point this out to clients *after* all the numbers have been done, resulting in a big editing exercise.

You can see in this example that only one item, 'office supplies', actually carries any VAT. Books are free from VAT and drawings are outside the scope of VAT. You, therefore, need to be careful only to include VAT on items on which you have definitely been charged VAT. If in doubt ask your supplier for a VAT invoice that clearly shows the VAT charge.

Overseas Issues

You have to provide information of purchases and sales made outside the UK on your VAT return. This applies to even the smallest VAT-registered business buying or selling overseas.

I generally recommend the inclusion of an extra column on your spreadsheets denoting the origin of the purchase or sale as 'UK', 'EU' or 'W' for worldwide.

Remember that EU VAT is not directly reclaimable on your UK VAT return and therefore European invoices are effectively treated as if the invoice has come from a non-VAT registered supplier in the UK, with no entry in the VAT column.

Figure 19.3 below shows a typical layout (the analysis columns have been dropped for simplicity).

Figure 19.3 Expenses Spreadsheet Including Overseas Purchases

No.	Date	Payee	Description	Origin	Gross	VAT	Net	Analysis >>>
1	05/01/2008	Staples	Office Supplies	UK	59.50	8.86	50.64	
2	06/01/2008	Taxcafe	Books	UK	24.95	-	24.95	
3	22/01/2008	Irish Ltd	Stock	EU	252.00	-	252.00	
4	28/01/2008	USA Inc	Stock	W	500.00	-	500.00	
					836.45	8.86	827.59	

Note the new column, 'Origin', denoting the source of the purchases.

- The first purchase from Staples is from the UK with full UK VAT applied.

- The second transaction, also from the UK, has no entry as there is no VAT on books.

- The third purchase from Irish Ltd (based in Ireland) is from the EU and although there is Irish VAT listed on the invoice, the total amount of £252 paid is the relevant figure. Irish VAT can't be reclaimed back directly through your UK VAT return, but you can use one of the VAT reclaim services mentioned above to do this for you.

- The fourth purchase of stock from the US carries no VAT. Sometimes VAT is added to imports from the US. This is normally because the importer is not VAT registered. If all your paperwork is in order this shouldn't happen, but if it does you can reclaim the VAT on your return as normal.

The same columns would also be required on the sales spreadsheet if you sell to overseas customers as seen in Figure 19.4.

Figure 19.4 Sales Spreadsheet Including Overseas Sales

Ref	Description	Date	Origin	Net	VAT	Gross	Date Paid
INV001	Mr A	01/01/2008	UK	1,000.00	175.00	1,175.00	23/01/2008
INV002	Mr C	02/01/2008	EU	250.00	43.75	293.75	
INV003	Mr X	05/01/2008	EU	500.00	-	500.00	
INV004	Mr Z	20/01/2008	W	800.00	-	800.00	
Total				2,550.00	218.75	2,768.75	

- The first sale to Mr A is a straightforward sale for £1,000 plus VAT.

- The sale to Mr C carried VAT even through Mr C is in the EU. This is because Mr C is an individual. You are obliged to charge VAT to other persons in the EU unless they are VAT-registered businesses.

- Mr X is also in the EU, but being a VAT registered business in France and having supplied a valid VAT number he is not charged VAT. Had Mr X not provided a French VAT number, VAT would have to have been included on this invoice, just like it was for Mr C above.

- Mr Z is based in the US and has no VAT added under any circumstances, as VAT only applies to sales within the EU.

If this is a bit confusing, it will help to go back to Chapter 6 and have a look again at the overseas issues.

This sort of formatting works if you have a small number of overseas transactions (or indeed only a small number of UK ones). If you have lots of transactions from all over the world (now quite common with website businesses), things might get more complicated.

You could perhaps keep a separate list of purchases and sales from the UK, EU and US by using separate spreadsheets, or it might be time to look at an accounting software package.

Chapter 20

How to Complete Your VAT Return

Even if you don't plan to complete your own VAT returns, it's definitely worth knowing how to do them. This way you will understand what information you need to collect on your spreadsheets and pass over to your accountant.

Let's look first at the layout of a paper VAT return and what data is required (see below). The first thing to note is that the VAT return is an extremely short document – just one page with nine boxes:

		£	p
VAT due in this period on **sales** and other outputs	**1**		
VAT due in this period on **acquisitions** from other **EC Member States**	**2**		
Total VAT due **(the sum of boxes 1 and 2)**	**3**		
VAT reclaimed in this period on **purchases** and other inputs (including acquisitions from the EC)	**4**		
Net VAT to be paid to Customs or reclaimed by you **(Difference between boxes 3 and 4)**	**5**		
Total value of **sales** and all other outputs excluding any VAT. **Include your box 8 figure**	**6**		00
Total value of **purchases** and all other inputs excluding any VAT. **Include your box 9 figure**	**7**		00
Total value of all **supplies** of goods and related costs, excluding and VAT, to other **EC Member States**	**8**		00
Total value of all **acquisitions** of goods and related costs, excluding and VAT, from other **EC Member States**	**9**		00

Basic VAT Return Example

Let's start with a straightforward example of a VAT-registered business with no international purchases or sales. I have listed all the boxes on the VAT return in Figure 20.1. Only the un-shaded boxes are relevant to this example. The shaded boxes deal with sales and purchases of goods to and from EC member states.

Figure 20.1 VAT Return Boxes

Box	Wording on the VAT Return	What This Means in Plain English
1	VAT due in this period on sales and other outputs.	The total VAT on your sales. Your output VAT
2	VAT due in this period on acquisitions from other EC Member States	Not applicable
3	Total VAT due (sum of boxes 1 and 2)	Add 1 and 2 together
4	VAT reclaimed in this period on purchases and other inputs (including acquisitions from the EC)	The total VAT on your costs. Your input VAT
5	Net VAT to be paid to Customs or reclaimed by you (Difference between boxes 3 and 4)	Box 3 minus Box 4
6	Total value of sales and all other outputs excluding any VAT. Include your Box 8 figure	Your sales before adding VAT
7	Total value of purchases and all other inputs excluding any VAT. Include your Box 9 figure	Your expenses before adding VAT
8	Total value of all supplies of goods and related costs, excluding any VAT, to other EC Member States	Not applicable
9	Total value of all acquisitions of goods and related costs, excluding any VAT, from other EC Member States	Not applicable

So what we need to come up with is:

- The total VAT on your sales (box 1)
- The total VAT on your costs (box 4)
- Your sales before adding VAT (box 6)
- Your expenses before adding VAT (box 7)

Using the basic sales information contained in Figure 20.2, we can quickly find the right data to include on the VAT return.

Figure 20.2 Sales Data

Ref	Description	Date	Net	VAT	Gross	Date Paid
INV001	Mr A	08/01/1900	1,000.00	175.00	1,175.00	23/01/2008
INV002	Mr C	02/01/2008	250.00	43.75	293.75	
Total			1,250.00	218.75	1,468.75	

We can see that the total output VAT (VAT on sales) is £218.75. This number goes in box 1 on the VAT return. The total net sales (sales excluding VAT) are £1,250. This number goes in box 6.

Excel Tip

We can also check that the figures are correct by multiplying net sales by the VAT rate (17.5%):

£1,250 * 0.175 = £218.75

Now this may seem a little farcical when dealing with just two transactions, but if you have 500 (or even 50) sales in the period it makes a lot of sense to double check the figures in this way. If we know that all sales carry VAT this figure should be identical every time.

In practice some sales may not carry VAT. But if your spreadsheet is telling you that the total VAT on your sales is £281.75, and the total net sales are £1,250 you would quickly see that this is more than the maximum possible VAT (£218.75). You would therefore hopefully spot the transposition error of the '8' and the '1'. This type of sanity check is good practice.

Expenses

Figure 20.3 Expenses Data

Date	Payee	Description	Gross	VAT	Net	Stationery	Books	Drawings	Insurance
05/01/2008	Staples	Office Supplies	59.50	8.86	50.64	50.64			
06/01/2008	Taxcafe	Books	24.95	-	24.95		24.95		
22/01/2008	Self	Drawings	105.00	-	105.00			105.00	
			189.45	8.86	180.59	50.64	24.95	105.00	0

The total VAT on costs (also known as input VAT) is £8.86 and goes in box 4 of the VAT return. Note there is no VAT on books and no VAT on money drawn out of the business (although drawings do feature in your records as an 'expense').

The figure used for total expenses before VAT (your net purchases) is not £180.59. We need to take off the drawings of £105, which leaves us with £75.59. This is the number that goes in box 7 of the VAT return.

Apart from drawings, other transactions that are outside the scope of VAT include bank interest, dividends and changes to directors' loan accounts, if the business is a limited company.

It is worth noting that even if you had included drawings by accident it wouldn't actually affect the amount of VAT you have to pay over to Revenue and Customs.

Your first VAT return (apart from my shading) will now look something like Figure 20.4

Figure 20.4 Completing the Basic VAT Return

Box No.	Description	£	p
1	VAT due in this period on sales and other outputs.	218	75
2	n/a	NONE	
3	Total VAT due (sum of boxes 1 and 2)	218	75
4	VAT reclaimed in this period on purchases and other inputs (including acquisitions from the EC)	8	86
5	Net VAT to be paid to Customs or reclaimed by you (Difference between boxes 3 and 4)	209	89
6	Total value of sales and all other outputs excluding any VAT. Include your Box 8 figure	1,250	00
7	Total value of purchases and all other inputs excluding any VAT. Include your Box 9 figure	75	00
8	n/a	NONE	
9	n/a	NONE	

The total VAT payable to Revenue and Customs is contained in box 5: £209.89.

Note the following:

- Where there are no figures to include (as in boxes 2, 8 and 9) write 'NONE' in the box rather than leaving it blank or putting a zero.

- Boxes 1-5 are completed using pounds and pence. Boxes 6-9 are completed using pounds only. Note that Revenue and Customs doesn't use proper mathematical rounding. So the £75.59 of expenses becomes £75.00, rather than £76 as mere mortals may have assumed. In practice it would take a rather pedantic tax inspector to get upset about such details but it always helps to make it look as if you know what you are doing when it's your turn for a VAT inspection.

The Importance of Timing

VAT returns are generally produced on a quarterly basis – once every three months.

You have to make sure you include the right invoices in the right VAT period. If you are using the accruals basis it's the date on the invoice that usually matters, not the date when payment is actually made.

For example, if your VAT period runs from January to March you have to include all sales and expense invoices that are dated January to March.

Some readers may be wondering whether they can manipulate their invoice dates to push VAT payments into later periods. Unfortunately Revenue and Customs is, as ever, one step ahead and has introduced something called a 'basic tax point'. What this means is they look at the underlying transaction to ensure you are not pushing things too hard.

For businesses with trading stock the relevant date is quite clear cut – it is the date on which the stock physically leaves your premises. For service businesses things get a bit more complicated but the 'basic tax point' is when you have completed the service.

You are allowed 14 days from this 'basic tax point' to get your invoice out, and the rules state that so long as you issue an invoice within 14 days, the 'tax point' is indeed the invoice date. If you haven't managed it within 14 days then the 'basic tax point' takes precedent.

Let's take a look at an example to clarify some of the points discussed so far.

Example

Margaret is a landscape gardener. Her current VAT return covers the three months from May to July. In July she has completed three jobs:

- *Harry – £200 for work carried out from 27 June to 5 July.*
- *Dolly – £300 for work carried out from 10 July to 18 July.*
- *An ongoing job for Helen at £500 per month, with invoices sent out at the end of each month.*

Now if Margaret sends out invoices at the end of the month for all three jobs her VAT payment will be £117.50 (£1,000 * 17.5%).

If she sends out her invoices on 1 August she may decide to include all three amounts in her next VAT return, covering the period August to October.

However, this isn't quite right. Harry's invoice for £200+VAT (£235) relates to work completed on 5 July, so the tax point is in July. The £35 VAT is therefore still due with the current VAT return, even though the invoice hasn't been sent out.

Dolly's invoice can be included in the next VAT period because there are fewer than 14 days between completing the job and sending out the invoice on August 1. This sort of adjustment makes things all a bit too complicated for Margaret's liking (she wants to be out designing gardens not worrying about VAT), so she vows to invoice everything within the month to keep it simple.

Margaret is, however, missing a trick. The ongoing job for Helen of £500 per month could actually be billed on 1 August, instead of 31 July, thereby deferring £87.50 of VAT to the next quarter.

If you do bill a lot of work on the last day of the month it can make a lot of sense to bill on the first day of the new month. However, you mustn't lose sight of the fact that we are only talking about *deferring* your VAT payments for three months, not avoiding the tax altogether. Most small businesses are more concerned about getting paid as quickly as possible rather than postponing their VAT payments.

Tips to keep your VAT returns simple

- Always send out your invoices on the same day you complete a job or send out goods.

- If you must wait until the end of the month to send out your invoices, make sure they are dated the current month and not the next month.

- For ongoing work, wait until the first day of the new month rather than the end of the old one.

If you follow this set of rules you won't have to think about it too much and will have more time to spend on your business.

Chapter 21

Overseas Purchases & Sales

It's time to look at a more complex VAT return with overseas purchases and sales. The overseas boxes only apply if you import or export **physical goods.** There is no need to separately report services that you may sell or buy in from abroad.

Figure 21.1 VAT Return Boxes

Box	Wording on the VAT Return	What This Means in Plain English
1	VAT due in this period on sales and other outputs.	The total VAT on your sales. Your output VAT
2	VAT due in this period on acquisitions from other EC Member States	n/a to most businesses
3	Total VAT due (sum of boxes 1 and 2)	Add 1 and 2 together
4	VAT reclaimed in this period on purchases and other inputs (including acquisitions from the EC)	The total VAT on your costs. Your input VAT
5	Net VAT to be paid to Customs or reclaimed by you (Difference between boxes 3 and 4)	Box 3 minus Box 4
6	Total value of sales and all other outputs excluding any VAT. Include your Box 8 figure	Your sales before adding VAT
7	Total value of purchases and all other inputs excluding any VAT. Include your Box 9 figure	Your expenses before adding VAT
8	Total value of all supplies of goods and related costs, excluding any VAT, to other EC Member States	Your total sales of physical goods to EU countries, before adding VAT.
9	Total value of all acquisitions of goods and related costs, excluding any VAT, from other EC Member States	Your purchases of physical goods from the EU, before adding VAT.

Boxes 8 and 9 are now filled in, although I am going to ignore box 2 as it seldom applies to most UK businesses. This box is used if you import from the EU but haven't yet paid for the goods. It's a bit complex but all you need to know is that in the worst case scenario you will end up with a timing difference (i.e. payment of VAT in the wrong period) rather than a total underpayment of VAT.

If your business is small enough to have manual records you probably don't have to worry about this point unless an inspector has told you otherwise.

So this time around we need to know a bit more detail:

- The total VAT on your sales (Box 1)
- The total VAT on your costs (Box 4)
- Your sales before adding VAT (Box 6)
- Your expenses before adding VAT (Box 7)
- Total net sales of physical goods within the EU (Box 8)
- Total net purchases of physical goods from the EU (Box 9)

You may like to note that the figures for boxes 8 and 9 are also included within the totals for boxes 6 and 7.

A summary of the sales is contained in Figure 21.2

Figure 21.2 Sales Spreadsheet Including Overseas Sales

Ref	Description	Date	Origin	Net	VAT	Gross	Date Paid
INV001	Mr A	01/01/2008	UK	1,000.00	175.00	1,175.00	23/01/2008
INV002	Mr C	02/01/2008	EU	250.00	43.75	293.75	
INV003	Mr X	05/01/2008	EU	500.00	-	500.00	
INV004	Mr Z	20/01/2008	W	800.00	-	800.00	
Total				2,550.00	218.75	2,768.75	

Total output VAT (box 1) is again quite straightforward being the total of the VAT column: £218.75.

The total sales before adding VAT (box 6) are also quite easy to find – the total of the net sales column: £2,550.

To get to the total net sales within the EU (box 8) we need to add up each sale with an 'EU' in the Origin column. In this case there are two transactions totalling £750.

A summary of the expenses is contained in Figure 21.3.

Figure 21.3 Expenses Spreadsheet Including Overseas Purchases

No.	Date	Payee	Description	Origin	Gross	VAT	Net	Analysis >>>
1	05/01/2008	Staples	Office Supplies	UK	59.50	8.86	50.64	
2	06/01/2008	Taxcafe	Books	UK	24.95	-	24.95	
3	22/01/2008	Irish Ltd	Stock	EU	252.00	-	252.00	
4	28/01/2008	USA Inc	Stock	W	500.00	-	500.00	
					836.45	8.86	827.59	

In this example the total VAT on costs (the input VAT) is again £8.86 and goes in box 4 on the VAT return.

The total expenses before VAT (net purchases) are £827.59 and go in box 7. There are no adjustments in this example for items outside the scope of VAT.

The net purchases from the EU are £252 and go in box 9.

The final VAT return looks like this:

Figure 21.4 Completing the VAT Return, Overseas Transactions

Box	Description	£	p
1	VAT due in this period on sales and other outputs	218	75
2	VAT due in this period on acquisitions from other EC Member States	NONE	
3	Total VAT due (the sum of boxes 1 and 2)	218	75
4	VAT reclaimed in this period on purchases and other inputs (including acquisitions from the EC)	8	86
5	Net VAT to be paid to Customs or reclaimed by you (Difference between boxes 3 and 4)	209	89
6	Total value of sales and all other outputs excluding any VAT. Include your box 8 figure	2,550	00
7	Total values of purchases and all other inputs excluding any VAT. Include your box 9 figure	827	00
8	Total value of all supplies of goods and related costs, excluding any VAT, to other EC Member States	750	00
9	Total value of all acquisitions of goods and related costs, excluding any VAT, from other EC Member States	252	00

Now this may all seem rather complex at first glance but if you work through the numbers a couple of times you should see that, if you record your income and expenses correctly, producing your own VAT return isn't all that difficult once you know how.

For further help, Revenue and Customs run quite good free courses for new business owners to help them get to grips with VAT and other aspects of tax.

If you can manage to set aside the time, a half or full day's training may be worthwhile.

Excel Tip

In these simple examples it has been easy to work out the EU figures. In practice it is probably somewhat more difficult. When preparing VAT returns for clients from their spreadsheets, I tend to copy the relevant data into a separate spreadsheet and use the Excel 'sort' function so all the UK, EU and W sales appear together. I can then easily total up the UK, EU and worldwide data. When carrying out 'sorts' it is always important to double check the total of the original data with the totals on the sorted data or it is easy to make a mistake.

Chapter 22

Pros & Cons of the Cash Basis

The cash basis for VAT is available to many smaller businesses. Rather than include income and expenses within your VAT return on the date an invoice is sent out or received, transactions are only included when payment is received or made. This is clearly of considerable advantage where a business has a lot of sales invoices that are only paid after a considerable time lag.

However, using the cash basis can make completing your VAT return a lot tougher, as the date of payment rather than the date on the invoice becomes important.

Let's look again at the sales records in the example we have been using:

Figure 22.1 Sales Spreadsheet

Ref	Description	Date	Net	VAT	Gross	Date Paid
INV001	Mr A	01/01/2008	1,000.00	175.00	1,175.00	23/01/2008
INV002	Mr C	02/01/2008	250.00	43.75	293.75	
Total			1,250.00	218.75	1,468.75	

On the right is the 'Date Paid' column. If we can account on a cash basis this becomes crucial, as only items for which payment has been received are included. Without re-working another VAT return we can quickly see that under cash accounting in this period we don't yet have to pay over the VAT on invoice 002 of £43.75, which represents a small but real cash flow advantage.

So far so good but in practice things get a bit harder once you have lots of transactions.

The main problem is that rather than being able to 'draw a line' between each accounting period and add up the data, you find yourself having to add up on a line-by-line basis the income and expenses that have come in or gone out between certain dates.

I like to follow a similar process to that outlined for determining whether sales are inside or outside the EU and UK and copy the data into a separate spreadsheet and sort by the 'paid date'. This is fine in theory but in practice the more manipulation you do, the greater the chance of error or omission.

As a rule of thumb I wouldn't generally suggest you persevere with cash accounting using spreadsheet software. If your cash flow is tight enough to make cash flow accounting worthwhile I would seriously consider the use of a basic accounting package that will do all these computations for you.

Otherwise your VAT return will turn into a quarterly hair-pulling exercise when instead you could concentrate on collecting some of these old debts.

Chapter 23

How to Benefit from the Flat Rate Scheme

In contrast to cash accounting, accounting within the flat rate scheme is pretty straightforward.

As you probably know, the 'standard' VAT rate is 17.5%. Under the flat rate scheme the tax rate applied to your sales when completing your VAT return is lower, so you have less output tax to pay Revenue and Customs. The flip side is that you are not allowed to claim back any input tax on your expenses.

Different businesses are allowed to use different tax rates, designed to leave them neither better off nor out of pocket using the system (although, of course, all businesses are different so some will be better off financially and some will be worse off financially). All businesses that use the flat rate scheme do, however, benefit from having a simplified VAT return.

Let's return to our familiar sales spreadsheet and assume that the business is allowed to use a VAT rate of 12% under the flat rate scheme:

Figure 23.1 Sales Spreadsheet

Ref	Description	Date	Net	VAT	Gross	Date Paid
INV001	Mr A	01/01/2008	1,000.00	175.00	1,175.00	23/01/2008
INV002	Mr C	02/01/2008	250.00	43.75	293.75	
Total			**1,250.00**	**218.75**	**1,468.75**	

You'll notice that the VAT rate used on the invoices is still 17.5%. In other words, when you send out invoices to your customers you still use the 17.5% rate as normal. The 12% rate is only used when completing the VAT return.

If this business is on the 12% scheme, we simply take 12% of the GROSS sales:

£1,468.75 * 0.12 = £176.25

This is the amount of tax paid over to Revenue and Customs.

You'll note that this is less than the £218.75 output tax appearing on the spreadsheet. However, it doesn't mean that this is a saving because no VAT can be recovered on any of the expenses of the business.

The difference between the £218.75 VAT charged on your invoices and £176.25 paid over is £42.50. This amount does unfortunately become part of your profit for tax purposes. In accounting terms it will be reported within your turnover figures.

The next change is what happens to the expenses spreadsheet. As you can see below we now totally ignore VAT and analyse the expenses on a gross basis, just as we did before VAT was included in the examples.

Figure 23.2 Expenses Spreadsheet

No.	Date	Payee	Description	Amount	Stationery	Books	Drawings
1	05/01/2008	Staples	Office Supplies	59.50	59.50		
2	06/01/2008	Taxcafe	Books	24.95		24.95	
3	22/01/2008	Self	Drawings	105.00			105.00
				-			
				-			
				189.45	59.50	24.95	105.00

This change does, of course, make your accounting easier.

The revised VAT return will look like the one in Figure 23.3. We simply show the VAT due in boxes 1, 3 and 5. There is no reclaim in box 4, nor any expenses shown in box 7.

Oddly, box 6 showing total sales, which normally contains net sales excluding VAT, contains *gross* figures. In other words it shows the total £1,468.75 you have invoiced your client, instead of £1,250.

Figure 23.3 Completing the VAT Return – Flat Rate Scheme

Box	Description	£	p
1	VAT due in this period on sales and other outputs	176	25
2	n/a	NONE	
3	Total VAT due (the sum of boxes 1 and 2)	176	25
4	VAT reclaimed in this period on purchases and other inputs (including acquisitions from the EC)	NONE	
5	Net VAT to be paid to Customs or reclaimed by you (Difference between boxes 3 and 4)	176	25
6	Total value of sales and all other outputs excluding any VAT. Include your box 8 figure	1,468	75
7	Total values of purchases and all other inputs excluding any VAT. Include your box 9 figure	NONE	
8	n/a	NONE	
9	n/a	NONE	

In this example the VAT due under the flat rate scheme is £176.25 compared with £209.89 due under the normal scheme. This is clearly a tax saving. Whether the flat rate scheme is right for *your* business is discussed in more detail in *Section 7 – How to Pay Less VAT.*

Chapter 24

How to Complete Your Return Online

Revenue and Customs has been putting a lot of effort into online filing and the services are generally good.

To find out how to signup for VAT Online Services type "VAT Online signup process" into Google and click on page returned from the hmrc.gov.uk website (the web page address is too long to reproduce here).

Signing up is relatively painless, although it does involve waiting to receive pin numbers which are posted out to you for security purposes.

The benefits of filing your VAT return online are:

- You have an extra seven days to file your return, plus probably another two or three because you need to allow time for a paper return to arrive in the post.

- You are less likely to make errors as the entries for boxes 3 and 5 are calculated automatically, and some basic checks are included within the software.

- The Revenue and Customs staff won't misread your handwriting or make keying errors. This can cause all sorts of problems when it does occur.

- Your return won't go missing in the post.

- There is a direct debit payment option so you can't forget to pay.

- Direct debit payments come out of your account on the 10th of the month, which gives you 10 days longer than a cheque payment and three days longer than an electronic payment with a manual return. Moreover if you normally pay by cheque you probably allow an extra few days for the cheque to arrive, so the real saving is probably closer to 14 days.

- Any repayments should be made more quickly.

Apart from a few minor grumbles about illogical layouts, I really can't fault the eVAT system and would strongly recommend using it.

Section 7

How to Pay Less VAT

So far in this book we have only considered the fact that either a business is VAT registered or it is not. For many small businesses the decision about whether or not to register is an important one. The aim of this section is to introduce you to some of the factors that can help you decide whether or not to register. We then go on to look at how to register for VAT and what special scheme options are available to you to make the accounting for VAT easier, and in some cases more profitable.

Chapter 25

Who Should Register for VAT Early

VAT registration is compulsory for some firms and optional for the rest.

Compulsory Registration

You probably know that compulsory registration applies if your annual turnover exceeds the VAT threshold, which is £67,000 for the tax year 2008/9. The basic rules are that you must register if either:

- At the end of any month your turnover in the last 12 months is more than £67,000.

- Your turnover is expected to exceed £67,000 in the next 30 days.

It is also possible to breach the threshold and not have to register, if you have a large 'blip' in your sales.

You can also deregister if you expect your turnover in the next 12 months to be less than £65,000.

You have 30 days to register after the threshold is reached.

You will then be registered from the first day of the second month after the month in which the threshold is reached. In plain English this means that if you hit the threshold in November, you have to register by the 30th December and start charging VAT from the 1st of January.

Please note this is a general summary, and there are quite a number of related rules and regulations that apply in some cases.

Voluntary Registration

You may choose to register for VAT even if your turnover is below the threshold. There are several reasons why you may wish to do this:

- **Credibility**. By registering for VAT you may look like a larger business than you really are. This can sometimes be helpful in winning customers in the early days.

- **Cash savings**. You will be able to recover all the VAT on your expenses (but read the comments below).

Generally speaking, if most of your clients are VAT-registered it makes sense for you to register too. Your customers won't mind having to pay VAT because they can recover it when they submit their VAT returns. You, on the other hand, will benefit from being able to claim back all the VAT you pay on your expenses.

If most of your customers are <u>not</u> registered then it may make sense to remain unregistered as long as possible. By charging VAT to unregistered customers you are effectively raising your prices, which may not be possible if you're in a price-sensitive sector.

If you register for VAT and your customers are not prepared to pay higher prices you will have to absorb the cost personally.

Let's look at some examples to see why the above statements apply.

Example 1 - VAT Registered Customer

Helen sells furniture to large businesses. She buys from VAT-registered suppliers and sells to other VAT-registered suppliers.

Let's look at a single transaction. Helen buys the furniture for £500 + VAT and sells it for £750 + VAT.

Helen's profit is simply £750 less £500 = £250.

Her VAT-registered customer is not concerned about paying £750 from a non-VAT registered company or £750 plus VAT because any VAT will be claimed back.

Had Helen not been VAT-registered her cost would have been the full VAT-inclusive price paid:

$$£500 + 17.5\% = £587.50$$

And her profit would be:

$$£750 - £587.50 = £162.50$$

This compares with profits of £250 if she is VAT-registered.

Alternatively, to keep her profits at £250, she could consider raising the price to £837.50. This is fine if customers are not sensitive to such increases but would normally result in less furniture being sold.

Helen concludes that, despite the extra paperwork, she is better off registering for VAT. She will also be able to reclaim VAT on office expenses and other business expenses as an added bonus.

Where most of your customers are not VAT-registered it's often better not to register voluntarily.

Example 2 – Non-VAT-Registered Customer

Helen's sister Sarah also buys furniture from a VAT-registered supplier but sells to private individuals rather than other VAT-registered businesses. She has seen how being VAT-registered increases her sister's profits and wonders if she could benefit in the same way too.

She buys the same item of furniture for £500 plus VAT, and wants to sell this for £875 to the end consumer.

If she registers for VAT she will recover the VAT on the purchase price and pay over the VAT on the sale. She works out the VAT on the selling price as follows:

Net Price	£744.68
VAT	£130.32
Gross Selling Price	£875.00

So as a VAT-registered trader she will sell at £744.68 and buy at £500 which results in a profit of £244.68. This sounds pretty good to Sarah and is equivalent to her sister's profit.

However, it could be even better if she wasn't VAT-registered. Her customers (the public) don't care if they pay £744.68 plus £130.32 VAT or just pay £875 with no VAT as it will cost them the same either way.

So if Sarah was unregistered selling at £875 she would pay costs of £587.50 on her purchase (£500 plus VAT) and therefore make a profit of £287.50. Sarah therefore makes the opposite choice to her sister Sarah above, making an extra £42.85 per sale, which is very welcome to her in the early days of her business.

Mixed Customer Base

Where a business deals mainly with VAT registered customers, registration tends to make sense, and where you deal mainly with the public, not registering tends to be favourable.

In the real world most businesses aren't usually so neatly compartmentalised, so this section is aimed at helping you work out what is best for you. If you get stuck, your accountant or business adviser can probably help you decide. The diagram below attempts to describe the decision-making process graphically.

Figure 25.1 The VAT Registration Decision

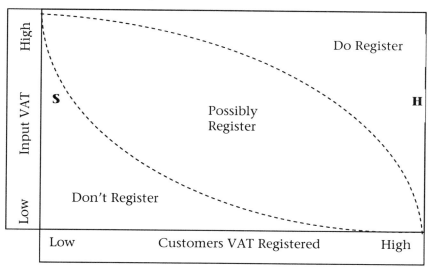

On the left is the input VAT of the business – the amount of VAT paid on expenses. The more expenses the business has, the more likely it will want to register to recover this money.

A small business providing *services*, such as a freelance journalist, accountant or consultant, will probably have very little input tax as there are probably few expenses that have VAT other than office equipment and some office supplies.

For example, for every £100 of sales there might only be £5 of costs that include VAT.

On the other hand, a business selling *products*, especially products with very low profit margins, will have high input VAT. For example, someone buying computer equipment for £90 and selling it for £100 will probably benefit more by registering for VAT.

On the bottom of the diagram we have the proportion of VAT-registered customers from Low to High, with low meaning most customers are unregistered.

The more VAT-registered customers there are, the more the business is going to benefit from registering because the customers will not mind having VAT added to their bills.

Let's look at where Helen and Sarah from the previous examples fit into the diagram.

All of Helen's customers are VAT-registered and her input VAT is medium to high. I say 'medium to high' because the purchase price of her products accounts for two-thirds of the sale price. She would appear roughly where the 'H' is marked on the diagram, implying that she should register for VAT.

None of Sarah's customers are VAT-registered but her input VAT is also medium to high, just like Helen's. Sarah would be over at the other side where the 'S' is marked, implying that she should not register for VAT.

In summary, looking at each segment separated by the dotted lines, in the left-hand segment we generally don't register where the proportion of VAT-registered customers is low and the input VAT is low. In the top right-hand segment the opposite is true. In the middle we have a large segment where it is unclear what is the best course of action and a little more analysis is required.

Now if you are still following this (and I appreciate that clearing out the gutters may suddenly seem very appealing) I would like to explain why the proportion of input VAT is a factor.

Do you remember Tom from our basic VAT example in Chapter 6? Last time we looked in on Tom he was chopping down trees and selling them to Dick.

Tom has very little input VAT. Apart from his chainsaw and a few other bits and pieces he has very few expenses that carry VAT. Tom would be in a similar position if he was providing pretty much any service with low costs, instead of selling products.

Now instead of selling all his timber to Dick who is VAT-registered, Tom starts selling half his output to the general public. Private individuals, not being VAT-registered, are just interested in the total price including VAT.

Let's say that during the year Tom sells £30,000 made up as follows:

- £15,000 to Dick plus £2,625 VAT
- £15,000 to the public plus £2,625 VAT
- Total sales £30,000 plus £5,250 VAT
- Total inputs are £2,000 plus £350 VAT.

He therefore makes profits of £28,000: £30,000 sales less £2,000 costs.

Now had Tom *not* been registered he could still have charged the public £17,625 as the total price they pay remains unchanged. This time, however, the total £17,625 excludes VAT and all ends up in Tom's pocket.

Dick will also only want to pay what he paid before which is £15,000 (remember he could recover the VAT paid so he really only paid £15,000).

By not being registered Tom will, of course, miss out on reclaiming the VAT on his purchases but we're only talking about a paltry £350.

In summary, without registering for VAT, Tom makes sales of £32,625 and has costs of £2,350 resulting in a profit of £30,275. That's £2,275 more than when he was VAT registered...not a bad return for a few back of the envelope calculations.

Looking back at the graph, Tom would be about half way along the bottom line and a little way up, falling squarely in the 'Don't register' part of the diagram.

Why Registering for VAT Can Be Beneficial

So much for businesses that have very little input VAT. If we move to the other end of the scale we will see that VAT registration can save you lots of money.

Harry, you may remember, bought furniture from Dick. Harry has just started a new business selling PCs and is VAT registered. His profit margins are very low – for every £1,000 of sales his cost price is £900.

Harry sells £30,000 worth of PCs during the year, made up as follows:

- £15,000 plus £2,625 VAT to VAT-registered customers.
- £15,000 plus £2,625 VAT to the general public.
- Total sales £30,000 plus £5,250 VAT.
- Total inputs £27,000 plus £4,725 VAT.

He therefore makes profits of £3,000: £30,000 sales less £27,000 costs.

He is making £100 profit per £1,000 of sales.

Now had Harry *not* been registered he could still have charged the public £17,625 because the price they pay remains unchanged. His VAT-registered customers would be unhappy about any increase so he would have to keep charging them £15,000.

Had Harry not registered he would therefore have made sales of £32,625 (£15,000 to the business customers plus £17,625 to private individuals). His costs would be £27,000 *plus VAT,* which he could not claim back, which comes to £31,725.

The final profit is therefore only £900, rather than £3,000 if he was VAT-registered.

If that wasn't bad enough, if you look at the sales to business customers, he is buying at £900 plus VAT (£1,057.50) and selling at £1,000. It doesn't take much business acumen to figure out that losing £57.50 per sale isn't a very good idea.

Looking back at the diagram above, Harry would be about half way along the bottom line and right up at the top, well inside the 'register' category.

From these examples we can see how being VAT-registered can either harm or benefit your business. We can also see that the VAT position can actually drive the type of business an organisation seeks.

If Harry wasn't VAT-registered he would have no incentive to sell to businesses at the prices given in the example and in practice would solve this issue by increasing his prices, which would presumably reduce demand.

VAT Registration Recap

Factors pointing towards early registration:

- High level of VAT registration amongst customers.
- High levels of input VAT (i.e. narrow margins).

Factors pointing toward delaying registration:

- Low levels of registration among customers.
- Low levels of input VAT.

In performing your own computations you should remember that you don't need a lot of accuracy to work out what to do, just a broad understanding of where you stand both now and where you are likely to be over the next 6 to 12 months.

If you perform computations along the lines of those in the above examples, rework the numbers several times, changing your assumptions. If the result comes out roughly the same each time then this should be good enough to make a decision.

If it is a close-run thing then it possibly doesn't matter much whether you're VAT registered or not. Generally speaking I would then err on the side of not registering as this will avoid the considerable extra administration effort required. You can see from the accounting part of this book that VAT makes bookkeeping somewhat harder.

Chapter 26

How to Register for VAT

Registering for VAT is a relatively straightforward process. You need to complete form VAT1. In theory it should take between three and six weeks for your application to be processed. Speeds vary considerably and it can take eight or more weeks if there is a backlog, especially if your business is in a 'risky' area such as the import or export of electrical items for which extra security checks will often be put in place.

To get this form either call the National VAT helpline on 0845 010 9000 or download the from the Revenue and Customs website. To do this type "value added tax application for registration" into Google and the first result from the hmrc.gov.uk website should be what you're looking for.

Alternatively you can apply online. To do this type "vat online registration service" into Google and go to the HMRC website. I recommend you click the FAQs link on this page as they answer most of the common VAT registration queries.

General Tips

- Use the online application form. This is somewhat easier to use than the paper version and it tends to get processed a little quicker.

- If you aren't sure how to answer a question on the form, check the website for help or ring the helpline – the staff are actually fairly well trained by helpline standards, although it can be worth calling twice to ensure they give you the same answer twice.

- If using the paper form make sure you provide a comprehensive answer to the 'Business activities' question (which asks you to outline your main and other business activities) – a one-line answer often results in further questions being asked.

- The bank account details can be added later if you are in the process of opening a business bank account.

- If your application is delayed, don't hesitate to chase it up with a call. Although HMRC claim otherwise, a significant proportion of clients with delayed registrations are active within 48 hours of a chaser call. If you don't hear from them call about a week before your intended registration date and then again on or just after the day on which you were supposed to be registered.

- Don't apply too far in advance. If you try and apply for a VAT number to commence more than 8 to 10 weeks in the future your application seems to get held back at HMRC's end. From my experience these applications do seem more likely to be delayed and need chasing up more than applications made around 4 to 6 weeks before the commencement date.

Chapter 27

VAT Schemes - Saving You Time & Money

There are a number of special schemes available to help smaller businesses. Sometimes they can appear confusing but are worth investigating because they can make a big difference to your cash flow, accounting requirements and the amount you pay over.

The following section outlines the various schemes available, the benefits, the problems and who should consider which type of scheme. Please note the turnover levels stated below exclude VAT, in other words are quoted as the total invoice value before any VAT is added. Full details are available on the HMRC website (type "Choose the right VAT scheme for your business" into Google).

Annual Accounting Scheme

What is it?

- You pay nine VAT instalments, which are estimates of your VAT bill, and a balancing payment at the end of the year. The first instalment is paid three months after the start of the year.

Benefits:

- Only one VAT return to complete each year
- Helps with budgeting your cash flow

Eligibility:

- Turnover on joining the scheme must be under £1,350,000.
- You may remain in the scheme until your turnover reaches £1,600,000.

Suitable for:

- Stable businesses with predictable VAT levels.

- Businesses where the owner wants an accountant to complete the VAT return at the same time as the accounts – one annual return should lower your costs rather than having four completed during the year.

Unsuitable for:

- Erratic businesses. If your turnover drops you may be left having to pay more VAT than you actually received. You can revise your monthly payments, but this may mean leaving the scheme and a lot of extra admin. If turnover rises you may end up with quite a big VAT bill at the year-end.

- Businesses with significant levels of investment. You may have to wait up to 12 months to reclaim the cost of large capital investments.

Cash Accounting Scheme

What is it?

- You account for VAT only when payments are made or received, rather than when invoices are received or sent out (the normal 'accruals' basis).

Benefits:

- You don't pay out VAT until you are paid by your customers. Conversely, you can't reclaim VAT on invoices until you pay them.

- Accounting can be slightly easier if you use the cash basis rather than the accruals basis. In layman's terms this means you can complete your tax return using your bank statements to determine your income and expenses, instead of having to use invoices that have been issued or received.

Eligibility:

- Turnover under £1,350,000 on joining.

- You may remain in the scheme until your turnover reaches £1,600,000.

Suitable for:

- Most businesses that have to wait to be paid, for example those with business customers. This can make a serious difference to your cash flow.

- People using basic accounting techniques. Some basic accounting software such as QuickBooks Instant only compute data for this scheme.

Unsuitable for:

- Businesses that receive payment soon after sale such as retailers.

- Businesses that pay their suppliers after they have been paid themselves. For example, if you get 90 days' credit on your purchases but get paid within seven days on your sales, this is likely to be unsuitable.

- Where you are likely to be receiving a VAT refund.

Flat Rate Scheme

What is it?

- Instead of computing your actual input VAT invoice by invoice, you ignore your expenses and calculate your VAT payment based on your turnover, using fixed rates.

Benefits:

- Easy to compute your VAT liability.

- Less emphasis on record keeping for VAT purposes.

Eligibility:

- Turnover under £150,000.

- Deregistration limit £191,489 net (£225,000 including VAT).

Suitable for:

- Many businesses when the flat rate percentage is favourable.

- Where your input VAT is relatively low.

Unsuitable for:

- Businesses with significant levels of exports that would not normally carry VAT.

- Where the fixed rates are unfavourable to you.

- If you have lots of investment spread over several small invoices under £2,000 as this will not be eligible for reclaim.

More about the Flat-rate Scheme

Unlike the other schemes, which are all about cash flow and timing, this scheme actually changes the amount of VAT paid over to Revenue and Customs, so it is quite possible to end up paying over more or less VAT. You therefore need to consider this scheme carefully.

In Appendix 3 you will find a list of the rates available to different industry types. Your particular trade may not fit neatly into this list, but you should be able to get some idea of the rate you would have to use.

The rates are all lower than 17.5% because you are not allowed to claim back any VAT on your expenses. The quoted rates are applied to your turnover only. Whether or not you're better off using this scheme depends on whether the lower VAT rate on your turnover adequately compensates you for not being able to recover

VAT on your expenses. What rate you use depends on your industry sector (see Appendix 3).

Probably the biggest point of contention about this scheme is that the quoted rates are somewhat deceptive.

For example, '11%' in this context means 11% of the invoice value *including* VAT, not 11% of the net invoice as most people would imagine at first glance.

For example, for a £1,000 + VAT invoice (£1,175 gross) the payment to Revenue and Customs will be £129.25 (11% of £1,175).

You may have expected to only pay over £110 (11% of £1,000). So '11%' really means '12.9%' when compared directly with the normal rate of 17.5%.

You will see in Appendix 3 both the headline rates and the effective rates. The headline rates are those supplied by Revenue and Customs. The effective rates were computed by me and are directly comparable to the 17.5% rate that most people feel more comfortable using.

Whether or not the flat rate scheme is suitable to your business is essentially a maths question, and it may help to refer back to the worked example earlier.

My clients tend to find the benefits relatively small because the rates Revenue and Customs let you use are broadly neutral and based on averages for each industry.

That said, for some businesses it can be quite an attractive proposition and is certainly worth considering.

Other Key Points to Note about the Flat-rate Scheme

- In the first year of VAT registration there is a bonus of 1% available. This means that if you would normally, say, be on the 11% rate you actually only pay over 10% until the first anniversary of VAT registration. This bonus is often helpful where there are higher expenses for a new company.

- Any 'profit' made using the scheme is taxable. In other words, if you have charged £1,000 in VAT in the period, but the flat rate scheme allows you to only pay over £800, the extra £200 you are keeping hold of will become part of your taxable profits.

- You can reclaim VAT on large capital purchases (over £2,000) in the normal way.

- This scheme can be used in combination with the cash accounting scheme.

- The deregistration test (£225,000 of turnover including VAT on a rolling 12 months basis) is performed on the anniversary of entry into the scheme. Therefore if you have a growing business you may not need to move back to the normal scheme right away.

Do seek advice if you're considering using this scheme. You may well need some help transferring between the normal scheme and this one. Moreover, I've had several clients who have used it for a few months and then transferred back as they didn't fully appreciate the rules and were losing money. This problem could have been avoided by seeking advice before making the switch.

Chapter 28

Clever VAT Registration Strategies

This section outlines some generic strategies that allow you to use the VAT system to your advantage.

Late Registration - Undercut the Competition

As we discussed before, where most of your customers are private individuals, registering for VAT is often not a good idea.

Take Roger, a legal executive who writes wills. None of his clients is VAT-registered and his input costs are negligible. Although Roger is good at what he does, he finds will writing is quite price sensitive. The local firm of solicitors charges £100 plus VAT, a total bill of £117.50. Roger considers four commercial choices:

- Register for VAT to appear larger than he is, charge £100+VAT (£117.50) and compete on service.

- Register for VAT and compete on price – say, charging £75+VAT for a total charge of £88.13.

- Don't register for VAT, but charge the same as the solicitors: £117.50.

- Don't register for VAT and compete on price, charging £75.

The following table shows the number of clients he estimates per month with each strategy:

Option	Price	No. Customers	Profit/Client	Total Profit
(1)	£100+VAT	10	£100	£1,000
(2)	£75+VAT	15	£75	£1,125
(3)	£117.50	10	£117.50	£1,175
(4)	£75	20	£75	£1,500

Clearly option (3) is the most profitable *per sale*. However, more money overall is being made with option (4) and Roger has to do twice as much work. As we can see VAT registration has made quite a difference to the business.

The main problem with this sort of approach is that the business model may get turned on its head if the business does really well and exceeds the VAT turnover threshold and is forced to register.

If this happened, Roger could either start to charge £75 plus VAT, which will lose him five customers, or perhaps consider selling at £63.83 plus VAT (a total price of £75), which will produce total profits of £1,277.

Either option looks quite unattractive when you consider how many more customers have to be handled. Roger may therefore choose to stay unregistered, sell at £117.50 so as not to spark a price war with the local solicitors and be happy to make £1,175 profit working part time.

In the real world if you attract customers by being cheap, you tend to lose them quite quickly when you put up your prices, so using this sort of strategy requires a lot of thought about where your business will be in the future. Staying 'niche' with a low turnover can often be a good alternative strategy.

Early Registration – Improve Your Cash Flow

Some businesses with high capital outlays, such as retail shops, will tend to have large expenses in the early months before much income has been earned. This is often financed through borrowing.

Although registration may not be compulsory for some months, reclaiming the VAT on the stock and fittings purchased could be extremely useful at a difficult time. It may therefore be worth opting for early registration to help the initial cash flow.

It is worth noting that the VAT on some start-up costs can often still be reclaimed when you eventually register, even if incurred up to three years earlier.

140

This applies to certain assets that are still in use but does not apply to stock that has already been sold by the time you register.

Selling Zero-Rated Supplies

If you are selling zero-rated supplies, for example if the majority of your customers are based outside the EU, then there really is little disadvantage to early registration. You can recover VAT on your expenses without having to change your selling prices as you won't need to add VAT to your sales prices.

Registering for Monthly Returns

If you are going to be claiming a VAT refund (for example, if you are making losses in the early days of trading or export much of your output) it may be worthwhile opting to complete a VAT return every month.

Although this may sound like a very bad idea from a paperwork point of view, receiving a monthly VAT refund from Revenue and Customs can be a real cash flow boost.

Temporary Registration

If you are running a business that is unlikely to breach the compulsory registration threshold you may find it beneficial to register for a short period of time, reclaim your input VAT on your start-up costs and then deregister.

There is some anti-avoidance legislation in this area, so this isn't something to 'try at home' – make sure you seek professional advice.

The main catch is that if you have assets on which you reclaimed more than £1,000 of VAT (i.e. total assets costing more than £5,714) you will have to repay much of the VAT.

Example

Ted is a window cleaner. He starts up and buys a van, ladders and other equipment. His total costs are £5,000 plus VAT. Ted expects to receive around £15,000 a year in sales to householders. Generally speaking, registration would be a poor option – his input VAT other than his van is negligible (and he hopes to keep this for at least five years) and none of his clients are VAT registered.

By registering in the first three months, Ted is able to reclaim the VAT on his initial costs, which comes to £875. Unfortunately he does have to pay over VAT of £558 on his sales in his first quarter, but still comes out £317 ahead. This is equivalent to more than a week's work for Ted, and he is understandably quite pleased.

Due to the way the rules are written Ted could have registered within three years of buying the van and still reclaimed the VAT, provided it was still being used in the business. However, by registering at the beginning of trading Ted knows that his sales are probably somewhat lower than they will be in 12 months' time, and he gets his VAT back faster when cash is at its tightest.

The sting in the tail, however, is that on deregistering Ted could have had to pay back the VAT on the capital equipment if the amount involved is more than £1,000.

For example, if the van cost £10,000 the input VAT recovered in the first tax return would have to be paid back on deregistering, thereby making this a waste of time. As I mentioned before, this sort of planning isn't something to contemplate without proper advice but it can work for some businesses, especially where there is lots of cost upfront.

Section 8

Other Issues for the Small Business

This section deals with some additional issues that affect many small businesses. In Chapter 29 we look at using Accounting Software as opposed to spreadsheets. In Chapter 30 I review the practical aspects of taking on your first employee and how to deal with the taxman. In Chapter 31 I look at how to get help with your accounting by employing a bookkeeper or accountant.

The Best Accounting Software

So far this book has focused mainly on using basic spreadsheets to do all your bookkeeping. Given that your objective should be to obtain the most information with the least effort, there's a lot to be said for doing it this way.

As your business grows, however, you may find that spreadsheets aren't powerful enough, unless the volume of transactions is quite small or you are quite diligent with your record keeping.

This is where using business software comes into the picture.

The main advantages of using software over spreadsheets are as follows:

- **Accuracy.** You are less likely to accidentally overwrite or delete data, and you remove the inherent risk of errors in formulas in your spreadsheets.

- **Management Information.** Even the basic reports produced by accounting packages tend to be a lot better than you can produce easily using a spreadsheet.

- **Instant VAT returns**. Some software packages can produce automated VAT returns once sales and expense information has been entered.

- **Speed**. Bank reconciliations and other accounting controls are generally quicker.

- **Stock Management**. 'Real time' stock information is available if you use business software.

- **Cost Savings**. You may save money when your accountant completes your tax return as he may receive better quality information from proper bookkeeping software than from your DIY spreadsheets.

The main disadvantages of using software are:

- **Your training time**. It is easy to underestimate how much time it takes to get used to a new software package. It may take you all day to get the software set up and several days training to get up and running. This is, of course, all time that you are not out there growing your business.

- **Garbage In/Garbage Out**. Just because the data is in the computer doesn't mean you have keyed it in correctly, set it up right or put it in the right place.

- **Processing time**. It may actually take longer to process each transaction in order to generate all the management information the software produces. And some of this information may not be very useful to a small business.

- **Flexibility**. Spreadsheets are by their nature infinitely flexible. You may not be able to do exactly what you want with some of the more basic accounting software packages.

- **Understanding**. If you don't understand the software it can be a lot more confusing than using the simple bookkeeping techniques outlined above.

Which Software Package?

The main providers of small business packages in the UK (and worldwide) are SAGE, QuickBooks and MYOB.

Each company offers various different versions of their software, ranging from the very basic entry-level version to the higher-end packages that have enough flexibility to be used by quite large businesses (100+ employees).

In the middle of the range are some sound products that are suitable for most owner-managed businesses. I would generally recommend you go for at least the package above entry level unless you are likely to stay very small. The entry-level packages are often not much more than an electronic cash book and most businesses quickly outgrow them.

For SAGE the minimum package to look at is Instant Accounts and for MYOB it's the 'Accounting' package. QuickBooks have unfortunately dropped their very good middle of the road "Regular" package and it's a toss up between the slightly too simple "Simple Start" and the slightly too professional "Pro" offering.

A new contender using an online system is KashFlow (kashflow.co.uk) and I have had several clients revel in its simplicity and user-friendly nature. The main issue with KashFlow and other similar online systems is the cost which slowly mounts up with ongoing subscriptions. Given bookkeeping doesn't change too much, a typical small client of mine may well happily use their same version of MYOB or Quickbooks for five years if they ignore their software provider's 'vital' annual upgrade.

As the marketing names seem to change rapidly, to avoid confusion, it's the packages priced at around the £100-200 you should consider purchasing, rather than those priced at around £50. Some of the banks give away free software from time to time but this tends to be of the 'cash book' variety and is best avoided, especially if there is a prolonged tie in.

Which to choose? Well most of the different brands do the job perfectly well although it is generally accepted that the newer entrants MYOB and QuickBooks are written more in plain English than SAGE, which can be rather 'accounting speak'.

Given they are all quite similar, I would suggest it makes most sense to buy the package your accountant or bookkeeper is most familiar with as you are likely to receive better quality ad hoc advice.

Also make sure all the features you want are available on the version you want to buy. For example, the ability to handle multiple currencies is important for many businesses, but not all middle-of-the-range versions have this feature.

Amazon.co.uk often has good prices for accounting software, although for higher-end versions of SAGE you may have to go through an authorised dealer (normally an accountant). Usually they'll have bought it a discount... so remember to ask nicely to have some of this passed on to you!

There are other packages around but these three give very good upwards flexibility, so you don't have to change your software as your company grows and its accounting needs become more complex.

A word of caution from my professional life; generally speaking, I find that where clients have started using accounting software before speaking to their accountant, a lot of time can be spent doing remedial work, taking apart bad working practices – so if necessary get help to do it right first time.

If you are ready for software you probably have a big enough business to warrant paying for a bit of professional help, and you should then get more out of your investment in terms of management information and data accuracy.

Chapter 30

Your First Employee

Not all small businesses employ someone from the start but in this chapter I outline the main practical issues when taking on your first employee.

The Basics

As you are probably aware, if you have been employed in the past, employers are responsible for the deduction of taxes from their employees before payment. This is called 'Pay as You Earn' (PAYE).

No doubt you've seen a big chunk of your wages disappear through income tax and national insurance payments.

What you may not realise is that, as an employer you have to pay another amount on top for 'Employers National Insurance'. The current rate is 12.8%. In other words, if you pay someone a salary of £1,000 per month you have to pay an extra £128 in national insurance.

The PAYE Process

The following is an overview of the system:

- **Registration**. All new employers have to register with Revenue and Customs. This includes sole traders, partnerships and limited companies.

  Note that if you are a sole trader without any employees, you are the 'proprietor', not an employee, and therefore don't have to register. The easiest way to do this is by calling the New Employers Helpline: 0845 60 70 143.

- **Set up**. Once you have registered with Revenue and Customs you will receive a large New Employers Starter Pack. In this pack is a form P46 (also available from www.hmrc.gov.uk/forms/p46.pdf) which you and your employee must complete and send back to Revenue and Customs.

- **Payslips**. Every month (or week if you are feeling particularly masochistic) you will pay your employee and hand across a payslip showing all the income tax and national insurance deductions you have made on their behalf.

- **Tax payment**. As a small employer you will probably only need to make quarterly payments of the income tax and national insurance you have been deducting, plus your payments of employers national insurance.

- **Annual Returns**. Once a year in May the total payments made are reported to Revenue and Customs through a series of annual returns. Your employees will receive a P60 summarising their total pay and tax deductions for the year, and a P11D if you provide any benefits such as healthcare or a company car.

Who Should Carry Out the Payroll?

Generally speaking I wouldn't advise any small business to run its own payroll for three reasons:

- It is a complicated and time-consuming process if you don't know what you're doing.

- It doesn't cost much to get an accountant or specialist payroll provider to do it for you. Some firms will complete a small payroll for as little as £15-30 a month (although watch the hidden fees!)

- Payroll is by its nature a sensitive subject. It's essential to have it processed correctly, so that you can explain to your employees why various deductions have been made.

Due to the bewildering number of obscure rules and regulations it is easy to make mistakes, especially with items such as sick pay, maternity pay, student loan deductions etc. If mistakes do occur most employers end up 'making good' any errors out of their own pocket, which could be costly. Even some accountants shy away from doing PAYE, unless they have an in-house specialist, as it's a full time job keeping up with all the rule changes.

Giving the job to a small payroll provider should only cost you a few pounds per month and will certainly save a lot of time and stress.

If you really want to do it yourself, then the best way is to follow through the instructions in the new employers pack step by step.

These instructions are quite good, and the free New Employer's Helpline is also staffed by pretty competent people.

However, don't calculate the deductions using the manual tables, use the CD-Rom provided instead. The software will get the deductions right so long as there is nothing too complicated involved (although the CD doesn't handle company directors properly which is a bit of a pain).

Some of the better accounting packages also offer payroll functionality, although this normally comes with an annual fee. One good value stand alone package worth looking at is Moneysoft's "Payroll Manager". Your year-end returns can be completed online as long as you register in time and most of the software packages are now integrated for online filing as standard.

Again this is a lot easier than using the manual forms, which bear all the hallmarks of civil service logic, and accompanying confusion!

General Tips for New Employers

- Get help interviewing candidates – a lot of recruitment companies will help you interview and select the best candidate for a role. If you only have one or two members of staff, selecting the best candidate for the role is vital to your new business.

- Get a proper contract. The rapid changes in employment law over the past few years have been significant and nearly all in favour of the employee. Having a good contract can save a lot of time and money in the event of a dispute. Don't be tempted to use something you find free on the web.

- Employer's indemnity insurance is not only compulsory if you have employees but can be very handy if, as a small business, you transgress some of the myriad of employment rules.

Contractors vs Employees

Given the level of red tape, the legal responsibilities and the cost of employing someone, lots of small businesses now prefer to use contractors rather than employ someone to carry out a specific task.

The cost tends to be higher but you should generally only pay for the time you use and there is no PAYE to worry about or additional taxation.

Contractors can be helpful when your business has seasonal peaks and troughs or just to add depth to a team where the business is too small to take on a full-time specialist.

The dividing line between employees and contractors can become quite blurred but there is often scope to define the relationship to give the desired result.

For example, let's say Raj needs a part-time secretary. He calls a local secretarial service and books someone for two hours a day.

However, sometimes there is no work to do and sometimes there is extra work available. Raj pays for the hours worked. One day the secretary accidentally orders 1,000 reams of paper instead of 10. The secretarial service agrees to sort this out with the stationery company for free as it was their employee's error. This sort of arrangement is indicative of a contractor relationship.

Raj's friend Colin also needs a part-time secretary. He places an advert in the local paper for a PA to come in for two hours a day.

He interviews three candidates and chooses the best one. If there is no work to do, he still has to pay the hours arranged. His secretary also has a bad day with the paper supplies but in this instance Colin has to pay overtime to cover time spent resolving the problem. This sort of arrangement is indicative of an employee relationship as Colin is taking on more of the risks of employment, rather than paying on a 'results' basis.

In these two examples it is quite clear cut who is who. In real life you may well need to take advice as to whether people who work in your business are contractors or employees.

Revenue and Customs scrutinise these situations quite carefully because there is potential to pay quite a lot less tax by defining a relationship as a contractor rather than an employee. In cases where it is found that the person really was an employee it is generally the employer who has to pay the additional tax. It is therefore very much in your interests as a small business to get the status clarified.

Chapter 31

How to Choose an Accountant or Bookkeeper

Throughout this book I have tried to point out areas where you may benefit from professional help. If you have never used an accountant before – and this probably applies to 90% of people with a new business – it can be daunting wondering what to expect, how much to pay and how to differentiate between different accountants and bookkeepers.

Accountants vs Bookkeepers

Q. What's the difference between an accountant and a bookkeeper?
A. About £100 an hour.

Jokes aside, this is actually a serious point. Although there is quite a lot of overlap between the two roles there are also some profound differences that may not be immediately apparent.

The bookkeeper will add up the numbers but a good accountant will know what numbers need adding up in the first place, and what to do with them once they are compiled. It is the difference between having an operational role and a management one.

Figure 31.1 shows the rough and by no means comprehensive division of tasks each will undertake.

A good bookkeeper will be diligent, accurate and quick. Moreover, good bookkeepers also know their limits. It's a 'good thing' if you ask your bookkeeper to do something and he or she tells you that an accountant normally does this particular task. This means they aren't trying to take on anything beyond their experience.

Most of the tasks covered in this book could be carried out by a good bookkeeper, although many would probably not be willing to help you choose a VAT scheme, for example.

Figure 31.1 Accountants vs Bookkeepers

Bookkeeper	Accountant
Day-to-day record keeping	Direct what records to keep
Input data into accounting system	Help you select accounting system, set it up and adapt to your changing needs
Prepare VAT and PAYE returns	Checking VAT and PAYE returns, and provide a point of contact to discuss new situations or trickier issues
Collation of records for the year end to pass to an accountant.	Preparation of final accounts, year-end adjustments, tax computation and returns.
Advice about keeping paperwork and other day-to-day issues	Broader advice about the direction of your business, things to keep an eye on, tax-planning opportunities. Buying or selling a business.

I would be wary if a bookkeeper offered help on tax matters such as completing your tax return, unless you have very simple affairs.

Nearly all bookkeepers will be able to competently transfer the numbers from your records into your tax return – the question is whether they are using the right numbers and understand enough about tax to do it correctly.

What bookkeepers are great for, however, is removing some of the drudgery of business red tape. A lot of people just aren't cut out to do this type of work and getting a good bookkeeper on board can result in a dramatic improvement in the quality of your record keeping and free you up to spend time on more productive tasks within your business.

I do, however, think it's important for every small business owner to keep a keen interest in their records, even if they are being looked after by a bookkeeper. This way you can keep a handle on how much you are spending, which customers haven't paid, what stock you have and other vital management information.

A good accountant will always make time for you, understand your type of business and the challenges you face. Small business owners often develop very close relationships with their accountants, who may be their only 'professional' adviser and business confidant.

Although one of the basic tasks for any accountant is to prepare your tax return and calculate the right amount of tax, this shouldn't be where the relationship ends.

The more effort you put into getting to know your accountant, the more you should get out of the relationship. I know from my own practice that I have very little input into the general business affairs of those clients I only speak to once a year. Those clients I have contact with on a regular basis tend to enjoy a far better level of service, as I am able to acquire a good understanding of their businesses. This way I can give timely advice and suggestions.

A quick two-line email to your accountant when something in your business changes will result in either reassurance that 'everything's OK' or immediate action. Where I don't see things until the end of the year, there is usually little time to be proactive – only time for damage limitation, which generally means more cost for the client.

Do I Need an Accountant?

There is no legal obligation to appoint an accountant, unless your business turnover is quite large and you need to have a 'statutory audit' carried out. The current audit threshold is turnover of £5.6 million.

Practically speaking, you should almost certainly get an accountant if you have a limited company or are VAT-registered. You may also benefit substantially as a sole trader, just from being able to sleep at night knowing that your records are in good order and your tax return has been accurately completed. In most cases your accountant will probably also save you a slice off your tax bill too.

Qualifications

Unfortunately, there is a bewildering array of professional qualifications in the accounting world. This is partly because, unlike solicitors, anyone can legally call themselves an 'accountant', and partly due to the failure of the various accounting bodies to form one entity.

Bookkeepers

Some really good bookkeepers are 'unqualified' or 'qualified by experience' (QBEs). This isn't necessarily a bad thing, especially for the mature person who may have trained years ago when passing exams wasn't as common.

Many bookkeepers who have trained in the past 10 to15 years will have studied for the 'AAT'. This is in four levels:

1. Bookkeeping Certificate (basic understanding of bookkeeping)
2. Foundation
3. Intermediate
4. Technician (Good rounded understanding of accounting)

Find out which level your bookkeeper has got to, as there is a huge gap from top to bottom. I would generally look for Intermediate or above as a mark of general competence to independently offer bookkeeping services.

Having said that, one of the most important qualities you should be looking for is experience in your type of business. Although it sounds harsh, a 'newly qualified' bookkeeper (or accountant for that matter) will be on a steep learning curve... rather let them learn on someone else's books!

Accountants

There are three major accounting bodies in the UK:

- ACCA – Association of Chartered Certified Accountants

- ICAEW – Institute of Chartered Accountants in England and Wales

- ICAS – Institute of Chartered Accountants of Scotland

These are the only three institutes whose members can call themselves 'chartered accountants'.

Members of these bodies will usually have the following letters after their names: ACCA, ACA, or CA. They may also have FCA or FCCA, with the 'F' standing for Fellow and indicating that the member has possibly more experience (although many experienced accountants don't bother applying to become FCAs or FCCAs).

As with every profession there is quite a bit of professional rivalry and snobbery. The ACAs tend to look down their noses at ACCAs. Quite frankly, it doesn't matter too much what type of chartered accountant you go for. They've all sat much the same exams and broadly will have much the same knowledge as each other.

There are several other accountancy bodies. The two main ones are:

- CIPFA – Public Sector Accountants (working in Government)

- CIMA – Management accountants (working in larger businesses)

It is rare for members of either of these two bodies to be 'in practice', offering their services directly to the public, and most would do the extra exams and be admitted to the ACCA if they wanted to switch career paths.

There are also a lot of other smaller bodies around, some of which don't ask for much more than an annual fee. However, I would question why one would want to use an accountant who is not a member of one of the mainstream bodies.

Opting for a chartered accountant ensures that your accountant:

- Has reached a high standard of academic study and is therefore reasonably bright.

- Has spent a bare minimum of three years qualifying and gained a further two years practical experience before being able to trade independently.

- Has studied a broad range of relevant material and has carried out mandatory ongoing training to keep up to date with new material.

- Has professional indemnity insurance, so you know that if you make a claim for bad advice they will have the funds to pay for your losses.

- Is subject to a good complaints procedure. Professional reputations are important for the institutes, and they therefore make a public show of ensuring accountants play fair and do a good job.

What you won't know is:

- The accountant's specific experience.

- What environment they trained in (for example, big business, smaller business, the public sector, manufacturing etc).

- How much they charge and on what basis.

- Whether you will get on with them personally.

- Whether your chosen accountant is any good, despite having the necessary qualifications. As with everything in life you get good and bad accountants.

Choosing an Accountant and Bookkeeper

Although you will get some idea of an individual's competence by looking at his or her qualifications, what this won't tell you is how enthusiastic, skilled or hardworking that person is.

As a rule of thumb you should choose an accountant with a business similar in size to your own. In other words, if you are a sole trader, there is little point asking one of the larger firms to act for you. They won't be used to small business issues, will charge a lot more and you are unlikely to get much one-to-one time with your accountant as 99% of the work will be completed by juniors.

Similarly, if you are a medium-sized business with several offices, you probably won't benefit from using a one-man band, as he is unlikely to have the resources or experience to cope with your needs. Instead use a medium-sized firm with experience dealing with similar sized businesses.

The next step is to ask around and see who has a good reputation and then set up a meeting, either on the telephone or in person. Most accountants will offer a free initial consultation to go over your affairs, and this is your opportunity to sound out their knowledge, experience and working practices.

Make sure you speak to several accountants until you find one that you get along with – remember you want to develop a long-term business relationship with this person.

Fees for smaller enterprises are increasingly being set on a 'fixed fee' basis. This means that you are being charged for a job to be completed, rather than on an hourly basis.

This tends to work well for routine paperwork such as completing tax returns but less well for the provision of advice where the scope may be less clearly defined. Advice tends to still be charged on an hourly basis and will usually be completed by one of the more senior members of staff.

Routine tax return work will generally be completed by either trainees or in-house assistants. Returns are then checked by an accountant before they are issued and discussed with you. Only in very small practices will the qualified accountant actually carry out all the routine paperwork.

The danger for a small business using a larger firm of accountants is that you may be pushed aside by bigger clients, which is why it is often helpful to match your business to the size of the accounting firm so you are always 'core business' and not on the periphery.

I should point out that some of the larger regional firms maintain very good small business departments, which can give the feel of a small practice despite being part of a larger firm. So explore what's on offer locally.

Once you have chosen a firm ask for all fees to be quoted in writing and check whether figures include VAT or not. You will probably receive an 'engagement letter' outlining the fees and terms for anything other than a very simple self-assessment return.

For hourly fees remember to ask for a fee cap – a maximum charge for a given piece of work. Although fixed fees may sometimes be negotiable, always bear in mind that accountants are selling their time, and if the fee is squeezed you may also find the service is squeezed too. Probably the most valuable service – tax planning and business support – is often the first thing to go with a cut-price deal.

Check-list for making an appointment

- ✓ Who is recommended?
- ✓ Do they hold relevant qualifications?
- ✓ Is it the right size of firm?
- ✓ Did they respond to my initial approach promptly?
- ✓ For larger firms, who will I actually be dealing with on a day-to-day basis?
- ✓ Do they have experience of my type and size of business?
- ✓ Am I happy with the fee structure?
- ✓ Am I 100% sure I get on with this person?

Dealing Day to Day with Your Adviser

It is worth remembering that your relationship with your accountant is a two way street.

Looking at it from the accountant's point of view, the following tips will help you get on with your adviser.

- **Keep good records**. If your records are poor, it will be cheaper to use a bookkeeper to sort them out than your accountant. Dumping a big pile of receipts on your accountant's doorstep will elicit a big groan and an even bigger bill.

- **Get in early**. Sole traders with a financial year ending in March, and tax returns not due until the end of January, 10 months later, often feel no sense of urgency to get their records over to their accountant. Remember, however, that accountants are very busy from November onwards, and many impose a 'busy season' premium for late delivery of information or discounts for early records.

  Not only will you probably pay more at this time of year, the quality of advice may be lower too as there is likely to be more time pressure on your accountant. If you get your accounts information together in early summer, you should find him only too keen to spend time working with you and some even offer 'early-bird' discounts.

- **Don't hold back**. Your accountant is there to help you. Everything you say will be treated in confidence – the more information you give, the better the advice that can be provided. Good accountants like communicative clients with whom they can get involved.

- **Respond to requests for information**. If you make your accountant wait weeks and chase you repeatedly for information it will ultimately result in higher bills – accountants make for an expensive diary reminder service.

- **Be realistic**. Although sometimes they can make your tax bill disappear, accountants cannot always perform such miracles, especially if you act first and ask questions later.

You should find that if you follow these tips you will end up with a positive business relationship which should mean in turn you get far better service in the longer term and better quality advice.

Headed Paper

The following notes outline the rules for headed paper. These vary depending on what business structure you have. Although there is no legal requirement to do so, I generally suggest to clients to treat their websites as an 'official document' and therefore include the same information.

For a sole trader you need:

- Your name (as proprietor)
- Any trading name
- Your trading address

If your trading name incorporates your name then this is not a problem. If I was a sole trader my trading name 'James Smith, Chartered Accountant' would be acceptable to cover both points.

For a limited company there is more information to include:

- You must include the company's full legal name
- Any trading names
- Where the company is registered i.e. England, Scotland or Northern Ireland
- Your correspondence address
- The registered company number
- The registered office address if different to your correspondence address
- Your VAT number if registered

Some of this information will quite naturally be included, i.e. the trading name and correspondence address. If you look at other people's headed paper you will probably see everything else in very small type on the bottom two lines. So long as it is legible this is perfectly acceptable practice.

My own footer for my practice runs as follows:

'James Smith, Chartered Accountant' is the trading name of James Smith (Accountant) Limited registered in England no. 4832439

Had my registered office address differed from my trading address I would simply add this in at the end to continue the flow.

Revenue and Customs Categories for Self Assessment

Table of allowable and disallowable expenses

(Taken from Self-employment (full) notes: Page SEFN 7)

Box No. Number Long(Short)	Allowable Cost	Disallowable Cost
16 (10)	Cost of goods bought for re-sale, cost of raw materials used; direct costs of producing goods sold; adjustments for opening and closing stock and work in progress; commissions payable; discounts given.	Cost of goods or materials bought for private use; depreciation of equipment
17 (18)	Construction industry subcontractor payments (before taking off any tax)	Payments made for non-business work
18 (12)	Salaries, wages, bonuses, pensions, benefits for staff or employees; agency fees, subcontract labour costs; employer's NICs etc.	Own wages and drawings, pension payments or NIC contributions; payments made for non-business work
19 (11)	Car and van insurance, repairs, servicing, fuel, parking, hire charges, vehicle licence fees, motoring organisation membership; train, bus, air and taxi fares; hotel room costs and meals on overnight business trips	Non-business motoring costs (private use proportions); fines; costs of buying vehicles; travel costs between home and business; other meals
20 (13)	Rent for business premises, business and water rates, light, heat, power, property insurance, security, use of home as office (business proportion only)	Costs of any non-business part of premises; costs of buying business premises

21 (14)	Repairs and maintenance of business premises and equipment; renewals of small tools and items of equipment	Repairs of non-business parts of premises or equipment; costs of improving or altering premises and equipment
22 (17)	Telephone and fax running costs; postage, stationery, printing and small office equipment costs; computer software	Non-business or private use proportion of expenses; new telephone, fax, computer hardware or other equipment costs
23 (18)	Advertising in newspapers, directories etc. mailshots, free samples, website costs	Entertaining clients, suppliers and customers; hospitality at events
24 (16)	Interest on bank and other business loans; alternative finance payments	Repayment of the loans or overdrafts, or finance arrangements
25 (16)	Bank, overdraft and credit card charges; hire purchase interest and leasing payments; alternative finance payments	Repayment of the loans or overdrafts, or finance arrangements
26 (19)	Bad debts written off. Amounts included in turnover but unpaid and written off because they will not be recovered	Debts not included in turnover; debts relating to fixed assets; general bad debts
27 (15)	Accountant's, solicitor's, surveyor's, architect's and other professional fees; professional indemnity insurance premiums	Legal costs of buying property and large items of equipment; costs of settling tax disputes and fines for breaking the law
28 (n/a)	Depreciation and loss/profit on sale of assets are not allowable expenses – any amount entered here should also be entered in box 43	Depreciation of equipment, cars etc.; losses on sales of assets (minus any profits on sales)
29 (18)	Other expenses. Trade or professional journals and subscriptions; other sundry business running expenses not included elsewhere; net VAT payments	Payments to clubs, charities, political parties etc.; non-business part of any expenses; cost of ordinary clothing

Flat Rate VAT Scheme Limits

Sector	Headline Rate	Effective Rate
Retailing food, confectionery, tobacco, newspapers or children's clothing	2%	2.4%
Membership organisation Postal and courier services Pubs Wholesaling food	5.5%	6.5%
Farming or agriculture that is not listed elsewhere Retailing not listed elsewhere Wholesaling agricultural products	6%	7.1%
Retailing pharmaceuticals, medical goods, cosmetics or toiletries Retailing vehicles or fuel Sport or recreation Wholesaling not listed elsewhere	7%	8.2%
Agricultural services Library, archive, museum or other cultural activity Manufacturing food Printing Repairing vehicles	7.5%	8.8%
General building or construction services Hiring or renting goods Manufacturing not listed elsewhere Manufacturing yarn, textiles or clothing Packaging Repairing personal/household goods Social work	8.5%	10.0%
Forestry or fishing Mining or quarrying Transport or storage, including freight, removals and taxis Travel agency	9%	10.6%

Advertising Dealing in waste or scrap Hotel or accommodation Photography Publishing Veterinary medicine	9.5%	11.2%
Any other activity that is not listed elsewhere Investigation or security Manufacturing fabricated metal products	10%	11.8%
Boarding or care of animals Film, radio, television or video production	10.5%	12.3%
Business services not listed elsewhere Computer repair services Entertainment or journalism Estate agency or property management services Laundry or dry-cleaning services Secretarial services	11%	12.9%
Financial services	11.5%	13.5%
Catering services, including restaurants and takeaways Hairdressing or other beauty treatment services Real estate activity not listed elsewhere	12%	14.1%
Architect, civil and structural engineer or surveyor Management consultancy	12.5%	14.7%
Accountancy or book-keeping Computer and IT consultancy or data processing Lawyer or legal services	13%	15.3%
Labour-only building or construction services	13.5%	15.9%

Pay Less Tax!

…with help from Taxcafe's unique tax guides and software

All products available online at **www.taxcafe.co.uk/books**

How to Avoid Property Tax
By Carl Bayley BSc ACA

How to Avoid Property Tax is widely regarded as *the* tax bible for property investors. This unique and bestselling guide is jam packed with ideas that will save you thousands in income tax and capital gains tax.

"A valuable guide to the tax issues facing buy-to-let investors" - **THE INDEPENDENT**

How to Avoid Tax on Foreign Property
By Carl Bayley BSc ACA

Find out everything you need to know about paying less tax on overseas property. Completely up to date with key UK and overseas tax changes.

Using a Property Company to Save Tax
By Carl Bayley

Currently a 'hot topic' for the serious property investor, this guide shows how you can significantly boost your after-tax returns by setting up your own property company and explains ALL the tax consequences of property company ownership.

"An excellent tax resource....informative and clearly written" **The Letting Update Journal**

Keeping It Simple
By James Smith BSc ACA

This plain-English guide tells you everything you need to know about small business bookkeeping, accounting, tax returns and VAT.

Property Capital Gains Tax Calculator
By Carl Bayley

This powerful piece of software will calculate in seconds the capital gains tax payable when you sell a property and help you cut the tax bill. It provides tax planning tips based on your personal circumstances and a concise summary and detailed breakdown of all calculations.

170

Non-Resident & Offshore Tax Planning
By Lee Hadnum LLB ACA CTA

By becoming non-resident or moving your assets offshore it is possible to cut your tax bill to zero. This guide explains what you have to do and all the traps to avoid. Also contains detailed info on using offshore trusts and companies.

"The ultimate guide to legal tax avoidance" **Shelter Offshore**

The World's Best Tax Havens
By Lee Hadnum

This book provides a fascinating insight into the glamorous world of tax havens and how you can use them to cut your taxes to zero and safeguard your financial freedom.

How to Avoid Inheritance Tax
By Carl Bayley

Making sure you adequately plan for inheritance tax could save you literally hundreds of thousands of pounds. *How to Avoid Inheritance Tax* is a unique guide which will tell you all you need to know about sheltering your family's money from the taxman. This guide is essential reading for parents, grandparents and adult children.

"Useful source of Inheritance Tax information" **What Investment Magazine**

Using a Company to Save Tax
By Lee Hadnum

By running your business through a limited company you stand to save tens of thousands of pounds in tax and national insurance every year. This tax guide tells you everything you need to know about the tax benefits of incorporation.

Salary versus Dividends
By Carl Bayley

This unique guide is essential reading for anyone running their business as a limited company. After reading it, you will know the most tax efficient way in which to extract funds from your company, and save thousands in tax!

Selling Your Business
By Lee Hadnum

This guide tells you everything you need to know about paying less tax and maximizing your profits when you sell your business. It is essential reading for anyone selling a company or sole trader business.

172

How to Avoid Tax on Stock Market Profits
By Lee Hadnum

This tax guide can only be described as THE definitive tax-saving resource for stock market investors and traders. Anyone who owns shares, unit trusts, ISAs, corporate bonds or other financial assets should read it as it contains a huge amount of unique tax planning information.

How to Profit from Off-Plan Property
By Alyssa and David Savage

This property investment guide tells you everything you need to know about investing in off-plan and new-build property. It contains a fascinating insight into how you can make big money from off-plan property... and avoid all the pitfalls along the way.

How to Build a £4 Million Property Portfolio: Lifetime Lessons of a Student Landlord
By Tony Bayliss

Tony Bayliss is one of the UK's most successful student property investors. In *How to Build a £4 Million Property Portfolio* he reveals all his secrets – how he picks the best and most profitable student properties; how he markets his properties and how he enjoys capital growth of 12% pa, year in year out.

Disclaimer

1. Please note that this guide is intended as general guidance only for individual readers and does NOT constitute accountancy, tax, investment or other professional advice. Taxcafe UK Limited and the author accept no responsibility or liability for loss which may arise from reliance on information contained in this tax guide.

2. Please note that tax legislation, the law and practices by government and regulatory authorities (e.g. Revenue and Customs) are constantly changing. We therefore recommend that for accountancy, tax, investment or other professional advice, you consult a suitably qualified accountant, tax specialist, financial adviser, or other professional adviser. Please also note that your personal circumstances may vary from the general examples given in this tax guide and your professional adviser will be able to give specific advice based on your personal circumstances.

3. Please note that Taxcafe UK Limited has relied wholly upon the expertise of the author in the preparation of the content of this tax guide. The author is not an employee of Taxcafe UK Limited but has been selected by Taxcafe UK Limited using reasonable care and skill to write the content of this tax guide.

Printed in the United Kingdom
by Lightning Source UK Ltd.
135309UK00002B/229-273/P